Bojan Žalec

Genocide, Totalitarianism and Multiculturalism

Philosophy in Dialogue
Philosophie im Dialog

Edited by

Prof. Dr. Janez Juhant
(University of Ljubljana)
and
Ass. Prof. Dr. Vojko Strahovnik
(University of Ljubljana)

Volume / Band 2

LIT

Bojan Žalec

Genocide, Totalitarianism and Multiculturalism

Perspectives in the Light of Solidary Personalism

LIT

Cover image: Anka Doblekar

This book is printed on acid-free paper.

Bibliographic information published by the Deutsche Nationalbibliothek
The Deutsche Nationalbibliothek lists this publication in the Deutsche Nationalbibliografie; detailed bibliographic data are available in the Internet at http://dnb.d-nb.de.

ISBN 978-3-643-90617-5

A catalogue record for this book is available from the British Library

Klosbachstr. 107
CH-8032 Zürich
Tel. +41 (0) 44-251 75 05
Fax +41 (0) 44-251 75 06
E-Mail: zuerich@lit-verlag.ch
http://www.lit-verlag.ch

LIT VERLAG Dr. W. Hopf
Berlin 2015
Fresnostr. 2
D-48159 Münster
Tel. +49 (0) 2 51-62 03 20
Fax +49 (0) 2 51-23 19 72
E-Mail: lit@lit-verlag.de
http://www.lit-verlag.de

Distribution:
In the UK: Global Book Marketing, e-mail: mo@centralbooks.com
In North America: International Specialized Book Services, e-mail: orders@isbs.com
In Germany: LIT Verlag Fresnostr. 2, D-48159 Münster
Tel. +49 (0) 2 51-620 32 22, Fax +49 (0) 2 51-922 60 99,
E-mail: vertrieb@lit-verlag.de

In Austria: Medienlogistik Pichler-ÖBZ, e-mail: mlo@medien-logistik.at
e-books are available at www.litwebshop.de

Acknowledgements

For the overall support in preparation of this book I would like to thank Valerija Japelj and Vojko Strahovnik.

I would also like to thank the Slovenian Research Agency (ARRS) for the financial support that enabled preparation and production of this book and for the overall financial support of the research project Religion as a factor of morality and intercultural dialogue (ARRS J6–6851).

Bojan Žalec
Postojna, November 2014

CONTENTS

INTRODUCTION

This book consists of four essays. At the beginning of this introduction let me quickly summarize their content. The first essay explains the concept of genocide by means of the concept of social death. Its central findings are the following: Genocide is an extreme form of social death. Intentional causing of social death is the central evil of genocide. Social death is what distinguishes genocide from mass killings. Physical killing of the members of the target groups is not essential for genocide. There are more sophisticated forms of genocide by which the members of the target groups are not killed physically, but there are rather destroyed "only" particular ties, relationships and social structures which are of vital importance for the survival of the target groups as such. The essay explains also what kind of groups are targets of genocide, the claim that genocide is an ethically laden concept, and some implications of this fact. On this basis it provides a comparative analysis of some phenomena closely connected with genocide: crime against humanity, totalitarianism, terrorism and ethnical cleansing. It reflects also upon the genocidal effects of military mass rapes. *What is genocide* is an important question. That's why it is very important to sharpen our minds for the recognition of genocide, also by providing an adequate definition of it which is appropriately tested. The last is the main aim of this essay which owes a lot to the work of Claudia Card.

The general aim of the second essay is to contribute to the answer on the question how studying of Kierkegaard could help us to understand societal and political life. I illustrate Kierkegaard's usefulness by example of an innovative and illuminative Bellinger's interpretation of Nazism and Stalinism given in Kierkegaard's terms of anxiety and stadia of existence. Bellinger interprets Hitler and Nazism as an extreme pathological example of the aesthetic stadium and anxiety before the good, and Stalinism as an extreme pathological example of the ethical stadium and anxiety before the evil. On this basis we may also speak about the importance of Kierkegaard for the understanding of depth motivation for political violence and crime.

The term *multiculturalism* bears many different meanings. The aim of the third essay, in which the influence of ideas of Larry Siedentop is evident, is to explain these different meanings. This is very important, as there are both positive and negative connotations attached to the term *multiculturalism*; hence, some forms of multiculturalism should be supported and others rejected.

A substantial part of the essay is devoted to the consideration of the damaging effects of some forms of multiculturalism on the democracy in Europe and on the future of the EU, in general. The role of Christianity is explained in relation to this subject. I explain the concept of identity. Identity is what binds people together and what at the same time distinguishes us from the others. For the cultivation of European identity (which is liberal) the consciousness that liberalism is a secular child of Christianity is necessary.

A considerable part of the essay is dedicated to elucidation of the utilitarian attitude towards multiculturalism and its implications. There is a similarity between utilitarianism and a special form of multiculturalism (levelling multiculturalism): as for utilitarianism all wishes are of equal value so for the levelling multiculturalism all cultures are equivalent. I warn against the dangerous phenomenon of Christophobia in Europe (Weiler 2003). In Europe we can notice the avoiding of recognition of truth about our own identity. That means that we neglect not only the truth about ourselves, but also the truth about the others. But is this really necessary to cultivate tolerance, coexistence, cooperation, dialogue, solidarity etc. between different cultures? I don't think so. True Christianity can be a foundation for tolerance towards others and for their respect. Therefore is Christophobia – which is based on the care for other, non-Christian cultures in Europe and when directed against genuine Christianity – unjustified.

In the last essay some general ideas and concepts of the theory of citizenship are introduced and presented and then applied to reflect on the specific situation in Slovenia. I pay great attention to three political virtues: civility, the capacity to object to the centres of power, and the virtue of public reason. The heart of the last is the capability of dialogue. In the contemporary Slovenian society those three central civic virtues are not sufficiently developed or cultivated. The essay is an attempt to contribute to the understanding of such condition by taking into account the Slovenian history. It focuses on the period from 1941 to 1990 (from the beginning of the occupation to the change of the regime (from the socialist one-party system to the liberal democracy)).

The reasons why I deal with the phenomena that are subjects of this book are various. Some are specific and some are of more general nature. The specific are connected with our Slovenian history and situation. In the WW II and after it Slovenia and Slovenians were subjected to Fascism, Nazism and Communism. There was a civil war and a lot of bloodshed. Genocide, totalitarianism, brutal violence, mass killings and other (related) crimes took place. In our small country – extended over only 20.000 km^2 – there is more than 600 hundred registered mass graveyards. In fact, long before 1941 Slovenes suffered under Fascism in Mussolini's Italy. We may say that Slovenes were the first victims of Fascism and its "guinea pigs". Slovene language was prohibited, Slovene children were extremely severely punished in schools because of its use, Slovenes were tortured and killed, their names were changed in Italian etc. Genocide started in its brutal and totally unhidden way. On July 13th 1920 the highly modern building of the Slovene national centre in Trieste was burnt down. Slovene writer Boris Pahor reports about his traumatic experience when he – as seven years old boy – observed Fascists dancing around the burning building like Indians. All this had happened twenty years before the WW II started. Immediately after the war extremely brutal and extensive mass killings happened in Slovenia in which tens of thousands of Slovenes and people of other nations were victims. After 1945 the decades of the Communist non-democratic regime followed. After the change of the regime no lustration at all was carried out, not even in its most limited extension and its mildest form.

The consequences – which are very present also in the present time – of such history are (uncured) traumas, psychological profiles and characters of many Slovenes which are unsuitable for free and democratic society, refusal to accept a truthful interpretation of the past, seriously damaged morality, lack of adequate work and business ethics, of democratic political culture, the positions of power occupied by non-democratically directed people who were part of the elite of the previous Communist regime (and by their "mentally" successors), and a strong polarization (cultural and political) of the Slovene society. The result is the crisis of the (contemporary) Slovene society and state – moral, economical and political.

Taking into account such situation it is not surprising that my colleagues and I are interested in topics like genocide, totalitarianism, terror, political crime, mass killings etc. and the ways of their preventing and overcoming of their effects. Among the last reconciliation, forgiveness, empathy, dialogue, solidarity and proper ethics of memory are especially worth to mention. All these topics are subject of intense research of me and my colleagues in the last decade (and even before). Our multidisciplinary research programs and projects are devoted to their investigation. A part of those investigations is published in this book. But these phenomena are of course not interesting only from the Slovenian point of view. There is no part and period of the human world which is not marked by genocide. Totalitarianism is far from being only Slovenian problem. Besides that – when we deal with such an extreme forms of evil like genocide and totalitarianism – a lot of things appear in much clearer way because they are not covered by usual compromises and concessions. They enable us to observe, intuit and recognize the essence of (evil) things in their "purest" form which is of immense value for philosophy, anthropology, ethics and other areas of knowledge.

All genocides are in this or in other form a kind of culturocide. So the question of proper relationship between different cultures is already from this point of view of big importance. Beside that modern world is globalized also in the cultural sense. Cultural heterogeneity is a fact in Europe and finding of the right attitude to this situation is one of the central European challenges. So, strong motivation for dealing with multiculturalism has many sources.

The view which I have named solidary personalism represents the background of all thinking in this book and the basic ethical measure. I explained it sufficiently in the essays in this book and in some my other texts so I won't repeat its explanation here. I only want to say a word or two about its origins and foundations. Christian faith and (intellectual) tradition, works of Kierkegaard, Franz Brentano, Emmanuel Mounier, Hannah Arendt, but also of Nikolay Berdiaev, Martin Buber, France Veber, Milan Komar, Eric Voegelin, Alasdair MacIntyre, Charles Taylor, Martha Nussbaum, Luce Irigaray, Martin Heidegger, Hubert Dreyfus, Emmanuel Lévinas, Zygmunt Bauman, Will Kymlicka, Wittgenstein and some parts of analytical philosophy are among its main origins, examples and inspirations.

This book is a philosophical book. I think that philosophy has two central and fundamental aims:

a) Introducing of new concepts and conceptual distinctions – without which our thinking is inferior and blind for sometimes even fatally important differences – and their fruitful application.

b) Checking, testing, controlling etc. of the correctness and grounds of our thinking.

These two tasks are mutually dependent because often you can prove that one's thinking is not correct or grounded only by introducing of certain (new) concepts or conceptual distinctions or by their fruitful application. I use this method also in the present book.

Let me explain my understanding of the job of a philosopher by a simple short story. One day a friend of my wife came to visit us. I started a conversation with her and she told me that there is a problem about which she wants to discuss with me. It was the following. She lives with her husband and her son in a really big house in the capital of our country where she works and her son is studying. Her son is twenty five years old. One day he came to her and let her know that he would move out of the house and would live alone – as a lessee – in a small bed-sitting-room. When she asked him what was the reason the answer was that he had enough of her control. This answer has really upset and affected her. She asked me what I thought. Is she really so possessive? Does she really interfere too much in his life? My answer was the following: I don't know neither you nor your son nor your relationship and your situation well enough to judge whether he is right or not. I am neither a priest nor your family psychoanalyst or psychotherapist. But I am a philosopher and I can help you and your son in a philosophical way to conceptualize your situation and to perform a dialogue on the problem.

I said to her that she should make some conceptual distinctions. The first is between control at one side and parental care on the other. The last is something good and it is parent's obligation to perform. On the other hand the first means managing the life of some other person instead of that person herself. As such it is something bad and a healthy person should resist it. An individual lives as a person in the full sense of the world only when she herself runs her life and not when it is ruled by somebody else. Otherwise her life is essentially impoverished. In such case she is in the substantial way not free. Of course a fully realized person who is not free is a *contradictio in adiecto*. A healthy personality should therefore resist and avoid any situation in which somebody else runs her life instead of her.

We may further make an additional distinction between supervision and control. In the case of supervision we oversee the situation but we don't interfere (though we can when needed). So for instance we can supervise traffic but we don't interfere in it.

Then I gave the following advice to my wife's friend: Use these concepts and conceptual distinctions and reflect the situation, your relationship with your son, your attitude toward him and your actions etc. Try to find out what actually they are: a control, supervision or just parental care. Your son should do a similar reflection. Afterwards you two should meet and discus, exchange and even argue in a dialogical way what you have found out.

She was pleasantly surprised by my – as she said – very original suggestion and she "promised" me to do that. I don't know how the story developed further because I haven`t met her since then.

This story in a simple way illustrates what is according to my opinion the fundamental task of philosophy – the conceptual equipment or enrichment of our thinking. This includes an analysis of concepts, introduction of new concepts and conceptual distinctions without which our thinking is inferior and (might be even fatally) blind for important distinctions. The aim of philosophy is also to provide an explicit understanding or definition of concepts as possible.

Let us illustrate this by a concrete example of genocide. An explicit understanding and definition of genocide is important in order to know whether we deal with genocide or not and for better understanding of its relationship to some other related phenomena belonging to other concepts: war crimes, crimes against humanity, ethnical cleansing, terrorism, totalitarianism, mass killings, mass (and systematic) sexual violence, etc. For that reason we must try to discern the concept of genocide from those concepts.

So the major part of the philosophical consideration of genocide is conceptual analysis of it and of relevant conceptual distinctions. These distinctions importantly enrich and enlighten our discussion. A debate without knowledge about those distinctions and their taking into account is necessary inferior. They enable us to see the important aspects of genocide which otherwise remain hidden, and nonetheless to recognize genocidal phenomena (as genocidal).

The fundamental method of the philosophy of genocide is therefore a (comparative) analysis of the concept of genocide. We can use also relevant (contemporary) literature on genocide and test findings and hypotheses in the light of concrete historical and contemporary phenomena. Of course we must take into account also legal texts which deal with the concept of genocide and other relevant concepts. But – on the other hand – exactly lawyers need philosophical elucidation of genocide in order to be able to better formulate their documents and do better job in general.

There are two essential moments of totalitarianism: ideology and violence. There is an analogous mistake we my commit by analyzing and defining totalitarianism and genocide. As I show in this book it is important that by definition of genocide we don't limit ourselves only to physical death. The essential moment of genocide is not physical death but rather social death. Physical death is only one (extreme) way to carry out social death. If we define genocide only by physical death then our definition doesn't cover some clear cases of genocide. We can notice a similar situation in the case of totalitarianism. If we limit our definition of totalitarianism only to the so called atrocious violence (or terror) (concentration camps, mass killings and arrests, physical torturing etc.) our definition leaves out some important (actual) cases of totalitarian regimes. The essence of totalitarianism is not only atrocious violence. Totalitarian aims can be reached also by "milder" forms of violence. The essential aim of totalitarian violence is to destroy persons as persons, to destroy people's autonomy, spontaneity, moral sense, responsiveness etc. Exactly such destruction of persons is the true nature of (totalitarian) violence. In essence it doesn't matter in what way it is achieved or tried to achieve: by atrocious violence, by propaganda, by advertising, by means of pills or some other chemical means; just as in the case of genocide it doesn't matter whether social death is achieved by way of physical death or in some other way.

On this ground we may explain the difference between totalitarian and post-totalitarian systems: while post-totalitarian systems are still totalitarian, the prevailing form of violence is non-atrocious, instead of atrocious. According to these definitions some regimes are not totalitarian in narrow sense of the word but they are still totalitarian in the sense of post-totalitarianism (Havel 1985; Killingsworth 2012). The examples of such post-totalitarian regimes are Communist states (in some of their periods) like Poland, DDR (Killingsworth, *op. cit.*) and Tito's Yugoslavia after 1950.

These examples nicely illustrate the importance of proper analysis and understanding of our concepts and hence of philosophy. If we are mistaken at conceptual level then we are mistaken on a very basic level and the consequences might be very serious. If we understand some concepts too narrowly some phenomena remain – in our thought – disconnected although they demand a common concept in order that our reflexion on them is adequate, fruitful and illuminating on one hand and not hiding or even leading astray. Our reflexion can increase our knowledge only if our concepts are adequate. In the opposite case it can seriously block it up and lead to mistakes.

Another general feature of totalitarian systems and genocides which we can discern from this book is that genocide, totalitarianism and even levelling multiculturalism are fundamentally anti-Christian phenomena. Maybe in the clearest way this is revealed by Kierkegaardian analysis of Stalinism and Nazism. This finding makes our book very compatible not only with Kierkegaardian, Weiler's and Siedentop's accounts that are explicitly used in this book, but also with such monumental narratives like Eric Voegelin's one or views of Pope John Paul II (2005) to mention just two distinguished examples. So for instance, according to Voegelin (1987) gnosticism – pace him modern totalitarianisms are just the extreme exemplifications of gnosticism – has two essential characteristics: imanentization and anti-Christianity. All these views converge to the finding that cultivation of the central elements of Christian anthropology, epistemology and ethics is of crucial importance for genuine liberal, humane and democratic society – in our modern, Western sense of these worlds – and that the negation or repudiation of Christianity is certainly not the right way to achieve this goal.

This book is just another small contribution to fortifying of this view. The first Vogelin's characteristic of gnosticism which was mentioned above – imanentization or elimination of transcendence – leads us to the fundamental bulwark against instrumentalism – and *eo ipso* against genocide and totalitarianism – the recognition of the transcendent nature of the world, persons, and human history. Recognition of transcendence is maybe not a sufficient condition to prevent extreme instrumentalist evils like genocide and totalitarianism but it is certainly actually necessary for not opening clear and wide road to them. At the bottom of depersonalization (both of a victim an of a perpetrator) which is described by authors like Arendt and Bauman, as the crucial element of genocides, totalitarianism, radical evil etc., lies the "elimination" of the transcendence of human person, its refusal or its negation. Or, as Luce Irigaray (2004, 8) wrote: without recognition of other's transcendence in flesh and spirit a true recognition of the other as the other is not possible. Recognition of one as a transcendent being and recognition of him/her as a person goes hand in hand. This principle sets a limit also to solidarity. We must strive for solidarity among persons (understood as mutual participation at their lives). Yet in this striving we should never forget that total participation is impossible. As soon as we forget this, our true recognition of the other as the other, as a person and the respect of his/her dignity is seriously endangered if not already destructed. Solidarity and transcendence of every person are the essential moment of solidary personalism. Therefore we may conclude that totalitarianism, genocide and also levelling multiculturalism represent the (extreme) violations of the ethics of solidary personalism.

At the end I would like to say few words about the level at which I deal with the topics in this book. This level is fundamental. If we analyse the conditions and factors – positive and negative – of genocide and totalitarianism there are many, various and at several levels. I limited myself to point to only some of them. The criterion was that they are fundamental enough to "deserve" philosophical attention. So this book tries to contribute to better conceptual understanding of the considered phenomena and to throw some light upon really fundamental origins, conditions and factors of totalitarianism, genocide and (harmful) multiculturalism.

GENOCIDE AS SOCIAL DEATH: A COMPARATIVE CONCEPTUAL ANALYSIS

1. Introduction

In this paper I deal with the concept of genocide. My main aim is to contribute to a better or clearer understanding of this important concept. I will try to do that by means of the concept of social death following – in this respect – in a substantial part the ideas elaborated by Claudia Card (2010).

The explicit understanding and definition of genocide is important in order to know whether we are dealing with genocide or not and for a better understanding of its relationship to some other related phenomena belonging to other concepts: war crimes, crimes against humanity, ethnical cleansing, terrorism, totalitarianism, mass killings, mass (and systematic) sexual violence, etc. For that reason I will try to discern the concept of genocide from those concepts.

In the major part of the paper I deal with a conceptual analysis and conceptual distinctions. Those distinctions importantly enrich and enlighten our discussion. They enable us to see the important aspects of our topic which otherwise remain hidden. The debate without knowledge about those distinctions and their taking into account is necessary inferior.

The main method I use in the paper is therefore a (comparative) analysis of the concept of genocide. I use relevant (contemporary) literature on genocide and I test findings and hypotheses in the light of concrete historical and contemporary phenomena. Of course I take into account also the legal texts which deal with the concept of genocide and other relevant concepts.

My own general and basic view – which provides the background of all my consideration in this paper – can be best described with the term *solidary personalism*. Solidary personalism can be maybe best understood when compared with nihilism and instrumentalism which form its antipode (cf. Žalec 2011a). Nihilism is a condition of an individual, a group, a society, culture in which experiential and intellectual horizons everything is leveled. A nihilistic subject cannot honestly experience one thing or being as more valuable than any other. As nihilism is practically impossible, it usually transforms into some kind of instrumentalism. Instrumentalism is the attitude that does not regard a particular person as a goal, but (at best) just as a means. To the contrary, for a personalist, every person is always a goal. The main aim of a personalist is flourishing of every person. Nihilism and instrumentalism are the fundamental problems (of our age). They seriously hinder or even stop the cultivation of dialogue, solidarity, approaching other as other etc. All mentioned goods and their relatives are essential moments of personalist attitude, ethics, relationships and existence. The fundamental (ethical) task (of our age) consists in (finding the ways for) the sufficient and adequate diminishing or limitation of the scope of the instrumentalist reason and practice.

The most appropriate attitude towards (cultural) identities might be called – using epistemological terms – critical realism (cf. Žalec 2011b, 112). Neither the attitude that takes identities as untouchable or overestimates their importance or superiority, nor the stance that diminishes their importance – or even considers them as something that should be destroyed or eliminated because they are only used for some bad aims, to instrumentalize people's attachments, affections, emotions for certain goals (political, economical…) – are proper. Neither the subordination of some individual concrete persons to some (collective) identity nor the "nihilistic" attitude to identity, are acceptable. Collective or moral identities[1] are necessary for the flourishing of persons, they have their irreplaceable value that should be respected yet they should also develop and transform themselves. Their good and acceptable elements should be accepted and some other parts should be discarded or modified.

One of the most central and basic background premises in this essay is that genocide (and other related phenomena with which I deal (crimes against humanity, mass murders, mass sexual violence, war crimes, totalitarianism) represents a violation of the ethics of solidary personalsim. Hence the negative/positive factors of solidary personalism are eo ipso positive/negative factors of genocide and of other above mentioned crimes. Similar thesis may be asserted – mutatis mutandis – regarding the correlations between nihilism and instrumentalism on one hand and genocide and its cognates on the other. Consecutively we may say that factors of solidary personalism/nihilism/instrumentalism may be considered

---

[1] For further elucidation of the concept of moral identity see Strahovnik (2011, 69–72).

as important factors and signs or indicators of genocide (or its cognate phenomena). Alas this essay would be far too long if we dealt also with the factors of genocides.[2]

There are two further topics which are very important for increasing the knowledge about genocides. The first is the sources of the information about genocides.[3] The second is (the elimination of) the (common) prejudices[4] about the factors, agents or elements of genocide(s). Neither of those two themes will be discussed in this essay. The reason is the same as in the case of the factors of genocide.

2. Definitions of genocide

2.1 UN Convention definition

The term *genocide* is not very old. It was first introduced by Raphael Lemkin in the 20th century. The international legal definition of genocide is given in the 2nd and 3rd article of the (UN) Convention on the Prevention and Punishment of the Crime of Genocide from 1948.[5] The 2nd article describes the psychical and the physical element of genocide. Both elements must be present in a crime that we can speak about genocide. The psychical element: intention to destroy (completely or partially) national, ethnical, racial or religious group as such. The physical element comprises five types of actions: a) killing of the members of the group (of a certain nation); b) causing severe physical or psychical damage to the members of the group; c) intentional exposure of the group to such life conditions which lead to its complete or partial destruction; d) establishing of measures with the intention to prevent new births in the group; e) forcibly transferring of children from one group to another. The destruction of groups, which is the aim of genocide, therefore does not mean

[2] For the factors of genocide see for instance Heidenrich (2001, 73–85), Jones (2011, ch. 16). I dealt with them in Žalec (2011c, 302ff).

[3] The sources of the information of genocide are considered in Heidenrich 2001 (74–79). Cf. also Žalec (2011c, 306–7).

[4] About prejudices and mistaken conjectures regarding genocide see Heidenrich (2001, 80–85), also Žalec (2011c, 304–305).

[5] The Convention is available on http://preventgenocide.org/law/convention/ (4th May 2011).

only killing, but also the destruction of the life conditions or factors of the group on economic, political, territorial, cultural and other levels or areas.

The 3rd article enumerates five types of criminal actions: a) genocide, b) a plan for the execution of genocide; c) direct and public promotion of the execution of genocide; d) an attempt of genocide; e) participation in genocide.[6]

It is important also to take into account the following words written by Claudia Card:

"So worded, the definition does not require that the intent succeed in destroying a group, even in part. Yet intolerable harm can be done if any of the enumerated acts is carried out. Any committed with the requisite intent is sufficient to ground a charge of genocide. The definition does not say explicitly that these are the only acts that might ground the charge. But neither does it provide a general principled way to identify other acts that might do so." (Card 2010, loc. 6368-77)

However, the definition of genocide from the UN Convention is deficient and insufficient. We can agree with the following citation from the journal *Zaveza:*

"As it can be seen from the definition formulated by the Convention of the UN, genocide means destruction of certain national, ethnical, racial or religious groups of people. Some think that political, economical and cultural groups are excluded since the Convention does not speak directly about them (compare the 2nd article). Anyway it is worrying that political, economical and cultural genocides are not taxatively enumerated, because there are not enough other international legal mechanisms which would protect from different regimes and repression those who think differently. Partly this gap was filled with the European convention about human rights[7] from 4th of November 1950 which is limited mostly to the European countries and therefore without real impact on the World situation."[8]

---

[6] Prim. http://www.preventgenocide.org/ba/pravnadefinicijagenocida.htm (4th of May 2011).

[7] Available at: http://www.media-forum.si/slo/pravo/pravni-viri/evropska-konvencija.pdf (4th of May 2011).

[8] http://www.zaveza.si/index.php/revija-zaveza/92-zaveza-t-04 (4th of May 2011).

2.2. The need for a broader definition of genocide

I also agree with Leo Kuper (1981; see also Jones 2011, 16–17) that the definition of genocide in the Convention of the UN is not fully adequate and that its biggest deficiency is that political groups are not on the list of those groups which are protected, since political differences are one of the most important reasons for genocides (beside racial, national, ethnical or religious).[9] Genocides against racial, national, ethnical and religious groups are – at least in many cases – results of political conflicts or they are at least closely connected with them. Nevertheless Kuper thinks that it is not good to change the meaning of the term which is internationally adopted and used. But because on the other hand such meaning of the term doesn't enable us to properly discuss the problem, Kuper has decided to use the term *liquidating or exterminating actions* against particular groups. I consider this term as not appropriate because it is too loose. So I will use the word *genocide* in the present text as referring also to destruction[10] of political groups and classes. At the same time I would like to add that we should think about the reason why the definition in the Convention of the UN is so deficient. Maybe just because it is true that political and class differences are so basic and allow the perpetrators of genocide to avoid charge of genocide saying: "We did not carry out genocide, we murdered on the basis of political and class affiliation and

---

[9] Also Chirot and McCauley (2010) wrote that the biggest genocides of the 20th century were ideological, not ethnical. I agree with this ascertainment yet we should know that things are very complex and that they are changing and that we should bear in mind also some other important facts as the following: "After the Cold War, ethnicity and religion came to be more important causes of conflict than ideology. Additionally, most post-Cold War conflicts were intrastate affairs involving some issues of autonomy for certain regions or groups. In a period of changing conceptions of national identity, many people involved in violent conflict began to identify with something closer to their daily experience than the nation, such as clan, ethnicity, or region, leading to a breakdown of centralized authority. Collective violence was characterized by factionalization and diffusion of power. Conflicts of this period did not in general lend themselves to mediation by existing formal and government mechanisms, including international law or precedent (based as it was in the state system)" (Lorey & Beezley 2002, xii).

[10] For completion of the survey of the accounts regarding the question "What is destroyed in genocide?" see Jones (2011, 29–33).

not on the basis of those which are enumerated in the definition of genocide in the Convention of the UN."

2.3. Lemkin's definition

Lemkin defined the term *genocide* – in his book *Axis Rule in Occupied Europe* (1944) – as denoting "a coordinated plan of different actions aiming at the destruction of essential foundations of the life of national groups, with the aim of annihilating the groups themselves." (Lemkin 1944, 79; quoted by Card 2010, loc. 6397–6403)

We can agree with Card that there is a certain – not unimportant – difference between Lemkin's definition of genocide and the one we find in the UN convention: "Unlike the convention, Lemkin does not understand genocide as consisting in any of a set of enumerable acts, *each* of which might have the intent to destroy a group 'in whole or in part.' Rather, Lemkin understands genocide as an overarching *plan*, and it is to the plan, rather to the specific kinds of action taken to implement it, that the requisite intent attaches. If the plan and its implementation are collective, so is the relevant intent. /…/ Activities that further such a plan take their genocidal character from that of the plan to which they contribute." (Card 2010, loc. 6403–13)

3. Forms of genocide

There are several forms of genocide. In scientific literature we can find many terms (cf. Jones 2011, 26–29): classicide, democide, ecocide, eliticide, ethnocide, femicide/feminicide, fratricide, gendercide, judeocide, linguicide, memoricide, omnicide, politicide, poorcide, urbicide.

So for instance the mass killings in Slovenia in spring 1945 were classicide (the term used by Mann (2005, 26)) or politicide[11] (the term used by Harff and Gurr; cf. Harff 2003).[12] Politicide is an intentional action in

[11] The Socialist Yugoslavia signed the Convention and ratified it. Its legal Code defined genocide as a punishable and imprescriptible crime against humanity. Also in the Legal Code of the Republic of Slovenia genocide is included and penalty prescribed for it.

[12] Alas also in the modern Slovene liberal democratic state a large group of people – more than 25.000 – was "condemned" to some form of social death. This is a group of the so called "erased citizens" who were in February 1992 erased

order to destruct a particular political social group. Barbara Harff and Ted Gurr think that "*revolutionary one-party states*" are the most frequent perpetrators of politicide (cf. Jones 2011, 28).

When researching genocides it is very important to take into account structural aggression or violence, that means destructive relationships which are a part of economic or social systems (cf. Jones 2011, 47). An example of such structural violence is poorcide (this term was first used by Udayakumar (1995) to describe genocide of poor people through structural poverty) which is carried out through neoliberal globalization. Anyway, researching of genocide should include the understanding of structural violence as a genocide mechanism. A large part of structural violence is a part of societal *background.* And this is exactly what we will do in the following part of the essay. We will focus our attention on the conditions of the vitality of groups. The destruction of those conditions is the aim of genocide.

4. Genocide as social death

A very important contribution to the understanding and defining of the concept of genocide has been given by the philosopher Claudia Card. The central role in her definition of genocide is played by the concept of social death: "Social death is not necessarily genocide. But genocide is social death." (Card 2010, loc. 5559–61)

In this chapter I will follow the understanding of the term social death as we find it in Card's book. Let us read the following quotation in order to better understand the way how she uses the term social death and its implied term social vitality:

"Social vitality is interpersonal. An individual can experience social death without others experiencing it, too. But for an individual to have

---

from the civil registry of the Republic of Slovenia. In July 2012 the Great Chamber of the European Court of Human Rights delivered its decision finding Slovenia in violation of the *European Convention on Human Rights*. Cf. Sebastian Kohn, Victory for Slovenia's "erased citizens" at the European Court of Human Rights, available at: http://www.statelessness.eu/blog/victory-slovenias-erased-citizens-european-court-human-rights (6th of February 2013) and http://en.wikipedia.org/wiki/The_Erased (6th of February 2013). For a more detail consideration of the case of the erased see Beznec (ed.) 2007 and Kogovšek Šalomon 2012.

social vitality, others must have it. I borrow the concept of social death from Orlando Patterson's work on slavery (Patterson 1982, pp. 5–9). Patterson argues that slavery, as historically a substitute for slaughter of the conquered in war, simply substituted one kind of death for another, social death for mass homicide. Slaves in the Americas who descended from kidnapped Africans were born socially dead, cut off from intergenerational social connections in both directions, past and future. They were, as he put it, natally alienated. In genocides, survivors experience social death, to a degree and for a time. Some later become revitalized in new ways; others do not. Descendants of genocide survivors, like descendants of slaves who were kidnapped, may be 'natally alienated,' no longer able to pass along and build upon the traditions, cultural developments (including languages), and projects of earlier generations." (Card 2010, loc. 6090–6100)

Social death can have several different origins (slavery, illness, banishment, self-chosen isolation …). It is not always something bad, it depends, but in the case of genocides we are dealing with social death which is evil. As Card put it:

"Genocide is an extreme of social death. The intentional production of social death in a people or community is the central evil of genocide. That is not only when genocide is mainly cultural but even when it is homicidal on a massive scale. Social death distinguishes the evil of genocide, morally, from the evil of other mass murders. Even genocidal murder can be understood as an extreme means to the primary goal of social death. Social vitality exists through relationships, contemporary and intergenerational, that create contexts and identities that give meaning and shape to our lives." (Card 2010, loc. 5567–72)

These relationships may be of more private nature (with keen people, coworkers …) or less personal and mediated by social institutions (educational, religious, political etc.) (Card 2010, loc. 5570–74) Loss of social vitality is a deep loss. Not all mass murders or killings have as its aim such a loss. Card cites as an example 1995 Oklahoma City bombing by Timothy McVeigh. "It was an atrocity, but not a genocide." (Card 2010, loc. 5574–77) And of course not all mass murders that have as its goal the loss of social vitality of individual victims are successful in really carrying out their aim. Here is the Card's example which confirms this thesis:

"The Czechoslovakian Jews of Terezin from the 'family camp' at Auschwitz who walked into the gas chambers singing the Czech national anthem and the Hatikva clung to their social as well as spiritual vitality to the very end /…/. Nevertheless, the Nazi genocide robbed them of descendants who might have shared it (Card 2010, loc. 5577–85)."

Taking into account the centrality of social death for genocide we realize that killing of the members of a target group is not essential for genocide. There are (more sophisticated) forms of genocide that do not physically kill the members of a target groups, but "only" destroy certain ties, relationships and social structures which are of vital importance for the survival of target groups: "Forcibly sterilizing the women or the men of a target group, or forcibly separating children from their parents for re-education to assimilate them in another group, can be genocidal in both aim and effect." (Card 2010, loc. 5584–90)

5. What kind of groups are targets of genocide

Genos in genocide is today widely understood as people (Card 2010, loc. 5773–76). But what kind of group is people? In order to answer this question Card uses the conceptual distinctions between aggregate, structural group and social group. These distinctions are based on the work of Iris Marion Young.[13] People is not just an aggregate, nor it is just a structural group. A structural group is "a serial[14] collectivity united by the relationships of members to externals, which gives them common interests" (Card 2010, loc. 5774–80).

So, as Cards noticed, the occupants of the Twin Towers on 9/11 – for instance – were not a people. Rather "[a] people is a social group in Young's sense, that is, a collectivity united by internal relationships and traditions, such as common language and practices. Relationships that

---

[13] Cf. Card (2010, Part I, Ch. 1, subchapter 3, 4 and Part II, Ch. 9 (especially subchapter 3)).

[14] The term *series* for a kind of social group was first used by Jean-Paul Sartre (1976). His example is people listening to the radio. Young used the term *serial collectivity*. Her example is women (see Young 1997). Serial collectivities are unified by externalities. In the case of women such externalities are – according to Young (1997) – sexual division of labor and enforced institutionalized heterosexuality. (Cf. Card 2010, loc. 1929–32)

constitute a people include connections in kinship and citizenship as well as cultural and social relationships created by such things as a common literature, cuisine, humor, and by sharing in the creation and maintenance of laws and traditions. These practices and relationships create the social vitality that gives meanings to the lives of members of peoples." (Card 2010, loc. 5782–87)

Therefore one might conclude that social groups are the proper targets of genocides. Yet the matter is not so simple. Today it is the holocaust which is taken by majority as the main paradigm of genocide. But what kind of group did the Jews – as the target group of holocaust – constitute? Certainly not a social group, but rather a biological group:

"[T]he target of the Nazi genocide was not defined consistently as either a social group (united by internal relationships) or a structural group (united by relationships to externals) but was something of a hybrid in that it included both people who self-identified as Jewish and people who did not although they bore a variety of relationships to people who did. The apparatus of the Holocaust targeted more than Jewish people when it defined 'Jewish' at least partly in terms of biological ancestry, rather than cultural heritage. A biological group is not a people." (Card 2010, loc. 5792–97)

We may further enlighten the nature of genocide if we compare different groups and events: the terror over gays and the extermination of gay communities in the third Reich, the massacre in Columbine High School in 1999, and the destruction of Ku Klux Klan. Card argues that we are dealing with genocide in the first case, and not in the third. What are her reasons for this claim?

In the first case the Nazis forced gays to wear discriminating pink triangles and they put them in the concentration camps. So they detached gays from their communities and relationships which gave meanings to their lives and shaped them. That was enough to cause social death of gays. Of course those gay-communities were not solid, stabile, multigenerational and multilayered in other respects as for instance in the case of the Jewish communities, but still they performed the function of shaping and giving meaning to lives of gays, the function of social vitality, so we may speak about a sort of genocide in the case of gays` destiny in the third Reich.

Regarding the second example Card doesn't give a definitive and explicit answer, but rather an answer by formulating a necessary condition of genocide. The correct answer on this question "depends on the nature, extent, and depth of the social vitality created by the ties uniting those who spent so much time in that high school. What contribution did that vitality make to the meanings of their lives?" (Card 2010, l. 5892–34)

6. Genocide is an ethically laden (and therefore in a sense relative) concept

What about Ku Klux Klan? Why is the destruction of Ku Klux Klan communities not genocide? They create the identities of people, they shape people's lives and give meaning to them: lives of some people wither – in a sense – after the destruction of those communities. The justification for the negative answer in the case of Ku Klux Klan can be put very shortly: "Forcibly imposed social death of a group is not genocidal if the group itself is an evil" (Card 2010, l. 5856–58).

Whether we are dealing with genocide or not in the case of social death of a particular group, it depends on whether the group in question is evil in itself, whether its basic principles, code, ethics as such promote evil: "The judgment that a group is an evil must be understood as the judgment that what basically defines the group is evil, that evil practices are so essential to it that they could not be eliminated without eliminating the group" (Card 2010, l. 5856–61).

And still another aspect of the evil of genocide – from the prosperity of civilization and humanity point of view:

"A presupposition of the evil of genocide might be that ethnic, racial, national, religious, and relevantly similar groups need to be protected in order to secure the potential for development of the goods of civilization of humanity. There is no such need to protect evil organizations such as Murder, Inc. A similar thought is found in Lemkin's Axis Rule" (Op. cit., loc. 5906–11). Card concludes:

"In sum, if social death is central to genocide, the concept of genocide does capture something that was not already captured by existing war crimes and crimes against humanity. Relationships internal to a group – cultural, political, educational, familial, linguistic, religious – that turn what might otherwise be an aggregate into a community are destroyed or seriously degraded. The harm members suffer is a loss of context and identity that give meaning and shape to their lives and would have given meaning to their deaths. That loss is not captured by previously existing war crimes or crimes against humanity. There is, further, a loss to humanity in the destruction of human potential /…/." (Card 2010, loc. 5923–31)

It follows from the above that the concept of genocide is ethically laden. In the last instance ethics decides what genocide is and what is not. Now we can understand why people refuse to accept the use of the term genocide to denote their activities even when they themselves describe them as extermination. Genocide is already by definition something bad, evil, while extermination is not. Extermination can be even something morally good in the case of extermination of something bad.

There are two losses which are specific for genocide (comprehended as essentially involving social death): 1. The loss of the context or community which gives meaning and form to the lives of the people who are victims or targets of genocide; 2. The loss of humanity because of the loss of (particular) human potential.

Whether a particular activity is interpreted as genocide or not depends on the moral evaluation of community which is the target of the activity: whether the community in case is itself evil, whether it can be converted, whether it has in itself the potential for good or evil, whether it should be protected or destroyed in order to cultivate or protect creation, production and development of the goods of humanity and civilization. Yet what people see as good or bad (in these regards) is (or may be) relative, their judgment and estimation differ. Therefore it shouldn't surprise us that also the views and judgments on whether particular activities and processes are genocides differ.

Thus for instance the extermination of class enemies for communists was not a genocide, many of the middle age Christians wouldn't say that the extermination of pagans or heretics was immoral (and thus was not a genocide), and for the Nazis the extermination of the Jews is not a genocide. Thus also in the cases of the extermination in the Old Testament according to many Jews and Christians we are not dealing with genocide because that extermination was commanded by God. What God commands can't be morally wrong. Moreover, what God commands is morally good and obligating, not obeying God's command is wrong. Keeping those people alive would mean disobeying God's command and would be therefore morally wrong. Of course, somebody can stubbornly insist on ethically neutral definition of genocide but this is not in accordance neither with our intuition (genocide is wrong by definition) nor by the legal definition of genocide which defines it as a crime.

Let me at the end of this chapter summarize my view, based on Card`s reflections, concerning the relationship between the concepts of social death, genocide and evil. Such a summary is needed in order to avoid some possible misunderstandings or misinterpretations.

In short, I think that an activity directed to a social group aiming at social death of the members of this group is evil and (hence) genocidal if the group in case is not evil in itself (in the Card's sense of the word) or if the protection of the group is necessary for the prosperity of humanity ('or' is not exclusive). Besides I think that if the group in case is evil in itself then social death carried out against it is not evil and (hence) not genocidal. But from all that it doesn't follow that if a group is not necessary for the prosperity of humanity then social death against it is not genocidal. Only the "fact" that a group is not necessary for the prosperity of humanity is not a sufficient reason for claiming that social death against it is not genocide. Moreover, I think that the fact that a group is evil in itself is not only sufficient but also a necessary condition for claiming that an activity directed against it aiming at social death of this group is not genocidal. Neither legal definitions nor moral intuitions – both suggesting that genocide is necessary morally wrong – force us to accept some other (additional) necessary conditions for social death being genocidal. It follows that any activity directed to social death of a group is genocidal if the group in case is not evil in itself. This last proposition implies that no group that should be protected for the sake of the prosperity of humanity is evil in itself.

I have established that the concept of genocide is ethically laden concept. This in itself doesn't mean that what genocide is and what it is not is relative since it doesn't imply that what is ethical and what is not ethical is relative. But it is a fact that very often the same activity – aiming at social death of the members of a group – is ethically differently perceived: some people find it moral and some people find it immoral. It follows – from our definition of genocide – that some people think that this activity is genocide and some other that it is not. So I am only claiming that what genocide is and what it is not is relative in this epistemological sense. I am not claiming that what is moral and what is not moral is relative in some objective sense and hence that what genocide is and what it is not is relative from some objective point of view. In fact I think that it is not. But this question is not of my concern in this paper.

7. Genocide and some concepts related to it

7.1. Crimes against humanity, terrorism, auto-genocide

In some measure the extensions of the concepts of crime against humanity and genocide overlay. But there is a difference: the aim of crimes against humanity is not to destroy – totally or in part – a particular group – as it is put in the Geneva Convention from 1948 – but rather to perform extensive and systematic offences against the target group. Genocides differ from war crimes in that that they are not limited only to the war time; they can take place also before and after a war, therefore also in the time of "peace". (Cf. Bassiouni 2003, 536)

There is no universally accepted definition of terrorism, but there is some wide consensus about its characteristics. Terrorism has social and political aims. The goal of terroristic blind and unpredictable violence is to undermine the norms of behavior, laws and ways of fighting, to frighten, destabilize, dehumanize, humiliate, demoralize etc. There are always three parts involved in terroristic attacks: attackers, victims of the attacks, and the third party for which the attacks are meant in order to frighten, destabilize etc. it. (Cf. Schmemann 2003)

In the case of genocides there is no such third party. Quite to the contrary: public knowledge about genocides is undesired. Perpetrators of genocides want to keep their deeds in secret. Maybe the best example demonstrating this thesis is Cambodia under the Khmer Rouge. First they banished all the strangers and closed the country almost hermetically.[15] Then the genocide could start and alas indeed it started. It took dimensions and forms which are almost beyond imaginable.

---

[15] Cambodia, Rwanda, Turkey (genocides over Armenians), mass killings immediately after the World War II in Yugoslavia, Darfur etc. provide the evidence for the thesis that too low or inadequate support provided by the international community is an important positive factor of genocide (cf. Heidenrich 2001; Žalec 2011c, 304) This is also the reason that the authorities that perform genocide usually try to close the country as much as possible (though they are never totally successful in that, there are always some information which overcome the barriers (cf. Heidenrich, 2011.)).

The events in Cambodia provide an interesting case for the conceptual analysis of genocide. Some experts think that we shouldn't denote them as genocide taking into account the fact that the Khmer were killing other Khmer. The perpetrator was not somebody else who tries to destroy other nation, ethnical or religious group or community – what is the definition of genocide according to the international law. Yet such a position contradicts to common reason and also to our understanding of genocide. The Khmer Rouge were performing not only massive killings among their own people but also a destruction of the foundations of Cambodian culture: family, religion (Theravada Buddhism), and village. They caused not only physical death of around one fifth of Cambodian population but also social death of many others who survived. Primo Levi (2003) used the word *auto-genocide* in the case of Cambodia which I find very appropriate.

7.2. Totalitarianism

Totalitarianism and genocide are closely connected because totalitarian regimes as a rule carry out genocides. This fact suggests a conjecture that the connection between the two phenomena is not coincidental. In this chapter I will present the explanation why totalitarianisms are genocidal.

There is a little agreement among theorists about the answer to the question what totalitarianism really is (cf. Maier (ed.) 2004; Martinjak 2010).[16] Still generally we may say that the term denotes social systems where the rulers control all areas of life in society and where no sphere of society is autonomous. The Soviet Union – especially under Stalin – and Nazi Germany are usually taken as examples of a totalitarian regime. Also Cambodia under the Khmer Rouge is a good example.

As said above, totalitarian regimes as a rule perform genocide, and our three examples provide a lot of thrilling evidence for this thesis. So we may reasonably conjecture that the relation between totalitarian societies and genocides is not just accidental. But how can we explain that?

A convincing explanation can be provided by using the theory of Franz Neumann (cf. Neumann 1964) which I apply in the explanation which follows. To understand every societal phenomenon we must take into account three factors or elements: economical, social and psychological.

[16] About the basic and general characteristics of totalitarian thinking see Juhant (2002, 42–43).

They must be considered in their mutual interaction and interdependence and always regarding their concrete historical situation. If we take examples of Stalin's Soviet Union or Hitler's Germany we must be aware that in both cases there was a big need for integrating the citizens to smooth away tensions and conflicts in society and to create some identity which would strengthen the dictatorship. In both cases we may say that neither there were present any economical interests which could integrate a sufficient part of population (and enable the other two goals) nor there were any such social relations. Nazis used the ideology of folk community, and Bolsheviks that of classless society. They were actually both delusions yet they both worked. In order to explain their efficacy we must deal with the psychological explanation in which the emotion of fear plays the crucial role. Fear was directed to some more or less imaginary enemy and concrete people were then denoted as concrete examples of that enemy. In Nazi Germany the enemy was called Jews and in the Soviet Union (and in communist countries in general) a class enemy. The Nazi movement activated fear of certain groups in society and directed it to destructive actions which were legitimized by the identification with the *Führer*. Similar things happened in Stalin's Soviet Union. The consequence was genocide or classicide. So we have the following elements which lead to genocides in totalitarian systems: the need for integration of citizens, smoothing away the tensions and conflicts in society and creating of some identity which could strengthen the dictatorship; the lack of sufficient economic or social factors for achieving of those goals; the presence of fear from social enemy (which is intentionally and systematically created and cultivated by the rulers); the identification with the leader which legitimizes the crime of genocide.

The paradox of these totalitarian systems is that on one hand they were not able to survive without enemy (which performed the integrating and other two functions) but at the same time they tried by all means to eliminate this enemy. However, this is not the only paradox which is connected with genocide. Let us turn to another one known from the more recent history.

8. Genocide, ethnical cleansing, and systematic mass rapes: sperm as a biological weapon

Ethnical cleansing is the use of force, terrorization or intimidation in order to chase away the adherents of some ethnical, religious or other group from a particular territory. Its aim is – by the means of killing, destruction, threats and humiliation – to render return or restitution impossible. So for instance in the time between April and August 1992 Serbs banished more than 700.000 Muslims from 70 percent of Bosnian territory. But such massive migrations and deportations are not new phenomena: Greeks were banished from Turkey and Turks from Greece, Serbs from Croatia between 1941 and 1945, Germans from Czechoslovakia, Palestinians from the occupied areas etc. (Cf. Cohen 2003, 123)

Ethnical cleansing is a wide concept which doesn't refer only to one but to more criminal acts or procedures. (Cf. op. cit., 124) In January 1993 the UN Commission of Experts handed over to the UN Security Council a report in which ethnical cleansing is defined as "rendering an area ethnically homogeneous by using force or intimidation to remove persons of given groups from the area". (Cf. Card 2010, loc. 6338–41)

It is mentioned that in former Yugoslavia ethnical cleansing was carried out by means of killings, torture, arbitrary arrests and imprisonments, extrajudicial killings, rapes and sexual aggression, imprisoning of civil population, intentional military attacks on civilians and civil areas, nonhuman destruction of property. The final report of the Commission from May 1994 adds also the following crimes: mass killings, maltreatment of civil and war prisoners, use of people as a shield, destruction of cultural heritage, robbery of private property, attacks on hospitals, medical personnel and places marked by red cross or red crescent. (Cf. Cohen 2003, 124)

James W. Nickel (2001) distinguishes between genocidal and non-genocidal forms of ethnical cleansing. But what is the criterion of ethnical cleansing being genocidal? According to Nickel a policy is not genocidal if it does not aim at mass killings. (Cf. Card 2010, loc. 6334–36) But this criterion is not sufficient. As Card wrote:

"[A] policy is genocidal if it aims at destroying (or foreseeably destroys) an ethnic, national, religious, or other appropriately defined group. If that can be done without mass killing, then ethnic cleansing by means of expulsion can, in principle, also be genocidal." (Card 2010, loc. 6336–38)

Further I agree also with the following sentences: "Removal of an ethnic group from a territory need not be genocidal if there is a decent chance that those expelled will survive to become re-established as basically the same group at other locations." (Op. cit., loc. 6341–44)

I will not enter in this essay into a thorough discussion in which concrete cases there really was such a decent chance since this would take us too far. I just note that in the case of Muslims from Bosnia I think that there was no such decent chance.

Let us now turn our attention to mass rapes as a means of genocide. In the last war in Bosnia many Muslim women were victims of rapes committed by Serbs. Those rapes were massive and systematic. They took at least three forms: 1. Serbs came, they publicly raped Muslim women and killed them; 2. Serbs came, they publicly raped Muslim victims and gone away. Next day they came back and offered Muslims to safely leave the territory; 3. Rapes took place in special rape camps where Muslim women were raped regularly and systematically, for a longer period of time, by many different men. They were raped with intention to make them pregnant. The victims were raped even after they conceived, to the time when the abortion was not possible any more. Then the victims were released often accompanied with the words: "Go and give birth to a Serbian child."

Some authors (cf. Card loc. 6363–66) think that all three forms of military rapes are genocidal. I am interested particularly in the third kind of rapes. The "paradox" by this kind of rape consists in the fact that the increasing of the members of a group was used as a means to contribute to the realization of genocide over this group. So there the question arises which we will deal with below: Are those rapes genocidal and what are the reasons for an affirmative answer? I say in advance that I think that the correct answer on this question is "Yes". So what are the reasons?

As first I think that we should recollect some characteristics of genocide which we have mentioned above. The first is that mass killings are not necessary for genocide to take place. It is enough that one destroys or attacks the life conditions or foundations of the group. These attacked foundations can be of political, social, economic, biological, physical, religious or moral nature (cf. Card 2010, 6421–24). Second, an action or a procedure is genocidal if it aims to destroy some group or if it foreseeably destroys it. Thirdly, (according to Lemkin's definition) in the case of genocide there is a plan to annihilate the target group. Let's consider now our question according to these characteristics of genocide.

Due to the work done by some Italian journalists – they provided the data from the meeting of the Serb army officers in a Belgrade suburb in 1991– we know that the Serb army officers coined the plan how to banish Muslims from Bosnia, i.e. how to carry out an ethnical cleansing. After the analysis they established "that the morale, will, and bellicose nature of their groups can be undermined only if we aim our action at the point where the religious and social structure is most fragile (quotation from the minutes of the meeting, quoted by Card 2010, 6287–91)." They realized that they can achieve that most effectively by directing their harming action to the Muslim women – especially adolescent – and children. "Decisive intervention on these social figures would spread confusion among the communities, thus causing first of all fear and then panic, leading to a probable [Muslim] retreat from the territories involved in war activity (another quotation from the minutes of that meeting, quoted by Card 2010, loc. 6290–94)."

So clearly there was a plan of achieving ethnical cleansing. Part of this plan was intentional pregnancies caused by rapes in rape camps. But as we see above ethnical cleansing as such is not yet genocide. At this point the concept of foreseeable consequences becomes relevant. It was quite clear that the group of Bosnian Muslims can't survive outside of Bosnia. So the rapes were also genocidal. The immediate aim was ethnical cleansing. But it was clearly foreseeable that the group of Bosnian Muslims can't survive such ethnical cleansing. So it was foreseeable that achieving ethnical cleansing de facto means achieving genocide.

There is another interesting (novel) element in this horrific story: the sperm used as a biological weapon. As Card (2010) explained, this weapon has important advantages compared to some other biological weapons (bacteria, viruses). For instance, it doesn't contaminate the territory as viruses or bacteria.

9. Conclusion

Let me at the end summarize what we have done in this essay. We have explained the concept of genocide by means of the concept of social death. Its opposite is social vitality. Genocide is an extreme form of social death. Intentional causing of social death is the central evil of genocide. Social death is what distinguishes genocide from mass killings. The physical killing of the members of the target groups is not essential for genocide. There are more sophisticated forms of genocide by which members of the target groups are not killed physically, but there are rather destroyed "only" particular ties, relationships and social structures which are of vital importance for the survival of the target group as such. We have explained also what kind of groups are targets of genocide, the claim that genocide is an ethically laden concept, and some implications of this fact. On this basis we have provided a comparative analysis of some phenomena closely connected with genocide: crime against humanity, totalitarianism, terrorism and ethnical cleansing. We reflected also upon the genocidal effects of military mass rapes.

What is genocide is an important question and we need an adequate definition to help us to recognize it. It has many different manifestations, many various faces, it takes many different forms, it is directed to many different groups, it uses different excuses, different masks and guises. It is rarely openly admitted by its perpetrators as genocide. Such variety of forms of genocide and its similarity to some other phenomena – which however are not genocide – is also the reason why an integral and comparative approach to genocide is needed in order to get the right definition of it and to test it sufficiently. I consider that an outline of such an integral approach is the main achievement of this essay. Another important aspect of the recognition of genocide is caught in the question whether the agents of genocide themselves recognize – or are able to recognize – genocide in their own actions. This is much more difficult because genocide is a negatively ethically laden concept. The importance of a correct definition of genocide for legal purposes is obvious.

The roots of genocide sponge on society and crisscross it. They are hard to recognize because they mask themselves with some honorable values, with directing of people's attention to outer enemy etc. That's way it is very important to sharpen our minds for recognition of genocide, also by providing an adequate definition of it which is appropriately tested. The last is the main aim of this essay.[17]

---

[17] My thanks go to Natalija Žalec for her comments of a version of the present text.

NAZISM AND STALINISM IN THE LIGHT OF KIERKEGAARD'S THOUGHT

"When the man saw Jesus in the distance, he ran up to him and knelt down. He shouted, 'Jesus, Son of God in heaven, what do you want with me? Promise me in God's name that you won't torture me!' The man said this because Jesus had already told the evil spirit to come out of him" (Mark 5: 6–8).

1. Introduction

A general aim of this paper – which is a philosophical text – is to contribute to the answer to the question how studying of Kierkegaard can help us to understand societal and political life. The foundation of good philosophy is introduction and explanation of concepts and conceptual distinctions without which our thinking is essentially – sometimes even fatally – impoverished because it is blind for important or even crucial differences between things. The most important (Kierkegaard's) concepts for this essay are anxiety and its forms (before the good and before the evil)[1] and stadia of existence (aesthetical, ethical and religious).[2] The other form of philosophical creativity, beside the introduction of important concepts and distinctions, is an application of them in order to throw light on certain phenomena. Also in this respect it turns out that Kierkegaard is very fruitful and useful for social and political thought.[3] I illustrate this with

[1] Regarding my understanding of Kierkegaard's concept of anxiety I owe a lot to Perkins (ed.) 1985, especially to the articles of Dunning and Hall. See also Repar 1998.

[2] For the stadia of existence see Rae 2010, especially pp. 83–90, also Hribar 1987.

[3] The approach in philosophy that I practice and defend might be in a certain measure denoted as aesthetic in the sense as this term is used by Kierkegaard scholar Jamie Turnbull (cf. Turnbull 2013). Yet this doesn't mean that I agree with Turnbull's refusal of the value and meaning of the philosophical interpretation and use of Kierkegaard. This is of course evident already from the present text. One of the moments of this disagreement is Turnbull's sharp mutual exclusion of philosophy and theology. I don't see why the interpretation of Kierkegaard shouldn't be at the same time philosophical and theological. That this is the Turnbull's position we can infer from particular places in his article as is for

the example of the American theologian Charles Bellinger who has given an understanding of Nazism and Stalinism in the Kierkegaard's concepts of anxiety and stadia of existence. (Cf. Bellinger 1992, 2001, 2010.)[4] Bellinger interprets Hitler and Nazism as an extreme pathological example of the aesthetical stadium and anxiety before the good, and Stalinism as an extreme pathological example of the ethical stadium and anxiety before the evil. On this ground we may speak also about Kierkegaard's importance for understanding of depth motivation for political violence and crime.

2. Being in faith versus being in sin: demonic and pharisaic violence

Societies in which the opposition to faith and love becomes dominant can be – following Kierkegaard – only non-democratic and non-free.[5] The

instance the following: "To move beyond the tradition of misinterpretation that consists in reading Kierkegaard as a philosopher we need to make the ethical movement to commit to history and, ultimately, to the necessity of religious or theological interpretation" (op. cit., 61).

If we take for instance Kierkegaard's approach itself as a paradigm or as a model (for a recent detailed analysis of Kierkegaard's method see Schwab 2012) then it seems to me that neither the exclusion of philosophical approach to certain texts or thinkers nor such a sharp mutual exclusion of philosophical and theological approach is justified (not to mention that Turnbull doesn't explain what he means by theological approach).

One of the main tasks of philosophy is introduction of (new) concepts and conceptual distinctions and their creative application. The criteria of the felicitousness of this introduction are the extent and quality of understanding to which they contribute. Kierkegaard's and other texts can be in this sense inspiring, useful and fruitfully applied regardless of our detailed ideas about the historical individual Søren Kierkegaard.

However this doesn't entail that the study of Kierkegaard from the point of view of cultural or intellectual history is not important. Quite to the contrary! What I claim is only that this approach to Kierkegaard is not the only important and fruitful and that the philosophical (aesthetical) use of Kierkegaard can be (and in fact is) also such. If this was not true then the whole large number of texts written about Kierkegaard which cultivate philosophical approach would be unimportant or even harmful. Is this Turnbull's position?

[4] From here on I will denote this interpretation with KB.

[5] A good basis for this claim is provided in the chapter titled "Kierkegaard's Ethics of Love and Incarnation" in Slootweg 2009. However, this thesis is actu-

extreme examples of such societies are Nazi and Stalinist societies. Their deeper origin can be understood exactly by means of Kierkegaard's concepts as has been convincingly shown by Bellinger. Anxiety before the good is the essence of what Kierkegaard names demonity. Anxiety before the evil is the essence of the attitude which Bellinger felicitously names pharisaic although Kierkegaard himself didn't use this term. Both demonity and pharisaity are potentially more or less violent. Therefore we may speak about demonic or pharisaic violence.

When we are anxious we have – according to Kierkegaard – fear of what we desire and we desire what we fear. Anxiety is "a sympathetic antipathy and an antipathetic sympathy". (Kierkegaard 1980, 42)[6] God calls man to become a self that is an active synthesis of oppositions: finite and infinite, temporal and eternal, freedom and necessity etc. Sin is despair (cf. Kierkegaard 1985). Despair is not allowing the synthesis to be realized. It is an active avoidance of becoming a self. On the other hand the way of faith is to allow that these polar oppositions coincide in one being. Hence the opposite of being in sin is being in faith (cf. op. cit.).

2.1. Kierkegaardian interpretation of Nazism

The essence of the demonic way of being is the anxiety before the good. A demoniac is pervaded by fear and dread before redemption which God offers in Jesus Christ. A demoniac is closed in herself and reluctantly discloses herself. That is why a demoniac is – according to Kierkegaard – unfree because for Kierkegaard freedom is constant communication and the word is what redeems.[7]

---

ally one of the main points of my whole essay. The present essay as a whole (including the references to Kierkegaard's own texts in it) is the "evidence" for it. I can't quote some particular locus from Kierkegaard's opus where he (more or less) literally claims this. But if we take into account Kierkegaard's central concepts, ideas and views this thesis (or interpretation) makes sense. I add the reference to Slootweg's essay only as additional information that also some other (respectable) authors share this account about this general moral that we can draw from the Kierkegaard's opus as a whole.

[6] Anxiety is strange power which grasps an individual. The individual can't get rid of it and at the same time she also doesn't want this. Cf. Kierkegaard (2012, loc. 1010–1013).

[7] The demonstration of the meaning of language, communication, openness and expressing in Kierkegaard is an essential part of the Hall's (1985) excellent ex-

A demoniac fears foremost his future transformation, becoming a self as it is called by God to become. In order to prevent this she desires to completely control her environment. A social form in which this social panic appears is a deification of state-nation which is a "holly" place of protection before the voice of God. For this reason Kierkegaard claims that the crowd is untruth.[8] Aesthetes can become demonic and if there are enough of them a danger of a demonic society appears. When an aesthete becomes demonic the solipsism in the root of the aesthetic stadium shows its real character as refusing of ethical responsibility. The Nazis are instances of the aesthetic way of existence. Nazism was a refusal of the Western liberal political philosophy in favour of the return to pre-Christian Germanic primitivism.[9] Regarding the relationship between Nazism and Christianity we should point to Freud's ascertainment that Nazi's hate toward Jews at the bottom is nothing else but their hate toward Christianity (cf. Freud 2013, loc. 1529–1533).

In the case of Nazism we deal with the refusing of the ethical sphere of existence. People transferred their moral responsibility to the demonic aesthete Hitler. The German state was thus left without conscience. Instead of conscience the thinking of German people was controlled by demons like "blood", "soil", "race" and "fatherland". (8: 4)[10]

According to Kierkegaard the root of sin is lack of inwardness. This lack produces extermination of the spirit and exactly this is the essence of the demonic because human spirit is created by God to be in a relationship

---

planation of Kierkegaard's conception of good, freedom, evil, sin, demonic life, life of faith, and his convincing demonstration of how unfounded the reproaches of individualism – addressed to Kierkegaard – are.

[8] Cf. Kierkegaard (1962, 113; 115).

[9] This claim fits well famous Heine's analysis of the German "spirit" (from his *Zur Geschichte der Religion und Philosophie in Deutschland*) according to which its Christian element prevents it to give birth to barbarism beyond all comparison. For Heine's view see Kossoff (1983, especially 125–126).

[10] Bellinger's book from 2001 *The Genealogy of Violence* is accessible also at Oxford Scholarship Online. I used this version (accessed February 24th 2013). When I refer to this book I use the following enumeration: the first number in brackets means a chapter in the book, the number after the semicolon refers to the number of page in this chapter in the PDF version of the book at Oxford Scholarship Online. Whenever there is alleged no name of the author and year we are dealing with the reference to the mentioned version of the book.

with the eternal. Inwardness is thus the eternity in man. The anxiety before the eternal is the demonic. The voice which speaks "Did you come to destroy us" (cf. Lk 4:34) is an immature self. For Kierkegaard a demonic man is a man whose first priority is to "protect" himself of God's mercy which is seen by an immature self as a "destructive" power. In her effort to evade the mercy a demonic personality tries to become a god of her universe. As her own god such a person defines good and bad as she herself sees them and tries to rearrange the whole world for her preservation.

A demonic person is afraid of future and tries to avoid the pain implied by spiritual growth. The society of demonic aesthetes yearns for a leader who will make it possible for them to avoid the "future". (8: 7–8)

If you want to mobilize a crowd it is crucial to give it an enemy against whom the crowd will fight and try to kill, i.e. destroy him. This was totally clear to Hitler. The immature aesthetes search for the draining for their resentment, wrath, indignation, violence that is present in them. The leader only gives them what they want. From the statements of the Nazis we can understand that the key element of the program of the Nazi's violence was to proclaim the Jews as incurably evil or harmful (8: 9). Hence they simply had to be exterminated.

Those who held their "enemies" as incurably corrupted express by this a firm commitment to maintain their own so far existing form of existence. A society which consists of such people creates a utopian ideology about certain social group which allegedly can't be included. The motor of political violence is thus an internal alienation of people from the eternal, spiritual, from God. Such a society was also the Nazi society which was a society of demonic aesthetes (8: 10).

Demonic aesthetes want to protect themselves from their "shadow"[11] which is not the shadow of their past but the shadow of their future. There is a need developed in them to attack their "shadow" as an external object. They look for scapegoats which are by their own subconscious represented as themselves as mature persons. If in a society there are enough of such aesthetes who hide from their own future then the central characteristics of such society becomes identification and killing of scapegoats. The society becomes an aggregate of depersonalized individuals who

[11] "Shadow" – in the meaning of the word as it is used by Bellinger – refers to I, me, myself as changed by the response to the call of God. Cf. Bellinger 1992.

avoid the possibility to become a true individual before God and for this reason kill the scapegoats. And this killing of the "other" is actually the manifestation of basic desire of aesthetes: to kill the possibility of their own spiritual growth. (8: 10 ff)

2.2. Kierkegaardian interpretation of Stalinism

The essence of pharisaism is the desire to detach one's own self from the sinful past, to cut, suspend the connection with it. An ethical person (in Kierkegaard's sense of the term) is aware that she is a member of a societal body to which she bears responsibility and duties which extend in time. She believes that she lives ethically and justly. She experiences herself as an ethically competent person whose maturity enables her to teach and bring up aesthetes to become mature and stable as she herself is. (8: 10)

As the aesthetical stadium can become a societal principle just as well can be the ethical principle embodied in a society. In the last case we get a society of ethical personalities in Kierkegaard`s sense of the word. They held themselves as better, superior compared to other groups of individuals who – according to their opinion – exist in a less mature way. They can develop a personality structure which Haufniensis from *Concept of Anxiety* calls "anxiety before the evil" (cf. Kierkegaard 1980, 113ff). As in the case of aesthetes just as well in the case of ethicians anxiety becomes an obstacle or blockade for development of the self, I. In such a case the ethician wants to control the process of creation by constantly comparing herself with the others who are worse or inferior then she is. It comes to her fixation on the evil of the other. This fixation originates in the ethician's fear of her own fallibility, incompleteness, capability for the incorrect, bad, immoral, sinful action. It is a matter of fear of the fact that I am just one of the members of the human race, only a faulty and deficient man who partakes also in the deficiency of his species and society. Bellinger in this sense speaks about the fear of the ethician as fear of solidarity with the human race. (8: 11)

According to Bellinger Stalinism is an example of the demonical form of the ethical sphere of existence. Egoistic, aesthetic individuals must be excluded in order to cleanse society of negative elements and that it can progress towards the utopia. An aesthetic demoniac thus attacks the shadow of her future and an ethical demoniac the shadow of her past. For an ethical demoniac the scapegoat subconsciously represents an immature egoistic person. The killing of it is in fact an answer to her own incompleteness and (moral) fallibility what actually means to her own humanity. An ethical demoniac tries to avoid awareness about her own sinfulness or incapability not to sin. (8: 12)

3. Conclusion

A part of the evidence supporting KB comes from a recognition that more or less only the persons who have "resorted" to some religion, i.e. spirituality[12], were able to speak out (publicly) about their horrible crimes. This is one part of the evidence supporting KB.

Besides that KB offers us an important insight in the difference between Nazism and Stalinism. This is the question which is still nowadays seriously considered by many people. Some of them claim that there is no important difference between the two. Both were the example of a movement which generated a totalitarian regime and caused horrible victims. But some of them – to the contrary – claim that there is an important difference for the communist movements – at least in principle – fought for noble goals while in the case of Nazism already the declared values are unacceptable.

What KB reveals us in this regard is twofold. On one hand we can see that also in the value starting points there are essential similarities. In both cases a group of people was stigmatized as incurably bad and was subjected to horrible, actually genocidal violence. Yet, on the other hand, Stalinism and Nazism are also essentially different in their conservative and "creative" direction respectively. While Stalinism in fact tries to cre-

---

[12] The relatively well known examples from the territory of ex-Yugoslavia are a participant in the Titoist massive killings after the Second World War, Serbian Simo Dubajić and a Slovene poet, intellectual and politician Edvard Kocbek. Dubajić has latter accepted the Orthodox Creed and was (because of this) capable of regret, repentance and public talking about the horrible crimes in which he took a part (cf. Dubajić 2006). A Catholic Edvard Kocbek was one of the first (ex-) members of the Yugoslav communist elite who publicly and with regret and repentance broke the silence about these killings and who also called the then communist powers to confess the guilt. Cf. Pahor & Rebula 1975; Inkret 2011; also Juhant 2010 (the chapter on Kocbek). For some data about the rather bloody Slovene and Yugoslav history under communism see also the last essay in this book.

ate a new man, Nazism tries to preserve or restore the old one. Therefore from the KB point of view the observation of Stéphane Courtois, the author of the famous *Black Book of Communism*, is not surprising. He noticed that the German society – despite all damage – has still existed also after the fall of the Nazi regime while the Soviet system practically totally ruined the Russian society (cf. Courtois 2007, 136).

KB therefore warns us that we shouldn't too quickly ascribe "avant-gardism"[13], i.e. the attempt to create a new man, to all totalitarian movements. We may certainly ascribe avant-gardism to communism, but this is questionable already in the case of Fascism (which is according to me not a totalitarian movement or regime), not to mention Nazism. If we follow KB, Nazism is a deeply conservative or, to put it maybe more precisely, restoratively directed movement. [14] At the bottom of the Nazi's "creation" of the new Reich and Nazi man lies restoration which aims to eliminate all forces which have led to the present (modern) situation.[15]

KB is illuminating also regarding the origins of totalitarian ideology. A necessary condition for a totalitarian thought is an opposition to Jesus' doctrine. The key and distinguishing moment of the last is his command that we must love all people, including our enemies. The love toward a being implies the desire for the existence of this being, not for her death, neither physical nor social.[16] Therefore an in-culturation and co-existence with other cultures – and not their destruction – is an essential and crucial element of the genuine Christian approach to the other.[17] On the other

---

[13] The term *avant-gardism* was used by Tzvetan Todorov who seems to be one of those who consider avant-gardism as the key element of totalitarian ideology. Cf. Todorov (2012, 35).

[14] This is another point where we can see how the goals of Nietzsche (for instance re-evaluation of all values, super-man etc.) differs from the Nazi's ideals.

[15] The already above mentioned (cf. n. 9) Heine's analysis of German "spirit" and anticipation of Nazism is compatible with this.

[16] That the essence of genocide is social – rather than physical – death was convincingly argued by the American philosopher Claudia Card (2010). See also the first essay in this book.

[17] Therefore we should be very careful and prudent – in the light of findings of KB – in relation to initiatives also in Christian circles themselves which (too) strongly stress the need for some kind of restoration, need for restoring some past relationships, criteria, social hierarchies etc.

hand, the characteristic of totalitarian movements is that they carry out genocide against groups that play the role of a scapegoat.[18]

Nazism and Stalinism are not only political phenomena. They are rather also strongly religiously marked phenomena. (8: 14) Without taking into account their religious aspect we can't understand them properly. KB is an important contribution to this account. Gandhi[19] wrote, in his autobiography (1987), that the one who claims that religion and politics are two separated things, doesn't have the slightest idea neither about politics nor about religion. I think that the same is true for democracy and violence. The depth origins of politics and violence are of (anti)religious and (anti)spiritual nature respectively. Also Kierkegaard's intellectual heritage offers support for arguing in favour of this hypothesis, for its deeper setting and understanding.[20]

---

[18] A contemporary philosopher – who deals with violence – associates immediately the term *scapegoat* with the work of René Girard. One of the tasks for the researchers of Kierkegaard's and Girard's opus (where there is still a lot of work to do) is a comparative analysis of both thinkers. Some part of it has been already done by Bellinger himself (1992, 2001, 2008, 2010).

[19] For the comparison of Gandhi's and Kierkegaard's conception of love see Gabriel 2011.

[20] I presented the drafts of this essay on several occasions: at the symposium on Kierkegaard in Ljubljana in June 2013, at the conference on genocide and suicide in Celje in November 2013, at my lectures at BISLA in Bratislava in December 2013 and at the Jagiellonian University in Krakow in March 2014. I thank for the questions and remarks from the public on those occasions. However, my special thanks for their comments of the versions of this text go to Mark Kleyman and Vojko Strahovnik.

MULTICULTURALISM, LIBERALISM AND CHRISTIANITY: SOME ELUCIDATIONS (CONCERNING EUROPE)

1. Introduction

Is the topic of multiculturalism really as important as many of us think? Let me answer this question by using the words of Mark Kleyman (2012):

"On 22 July 2011 seventy-six persons were killed in Norway, and many of them were under the age of 18. A certain man decided that the practices founded in the idea of tolerance and multiculturalism threatened Europe, and a 'right' of defending European culture would justify any means of reaching it."

The term *multiculturalism* bears many different meanings. The aim of this paper is to explain these different meanings. This is very important, as there are both positive and negative connotations attached to the term *multiculturalism*; hence, some forms of multicullturalism should be supported and others rejected.

A substantial part of this paper is devoted to the consideration of the damaging effects of some forms of multiculturalism on the democracy in Europe and on the future of the EU, in general. The role of the Christianity will be explained in relation to this subject, while a considerable part of the paper is dedicated to elucidation of the utilitarian attitude towards multiculturalism and its implications.

This paper aims to be a philosophical text. This implies that the methods used are philosophical. More specifically, a lot of attention is paid to conceptual analysis and conceptual distinctions. These distinctions significantly enrich and enlighten the discourse on this subject. They enable us to see some crucial aspects which otherwise would remain hidden. A debate without the awareness of these distinctions and their consideration is inevitably inferior. To discover, explain and productively employ such distinctions is fundamental and probably the most important philosophical task.

The problems concerning the immigrant groups, cultural minorities, and fundamentalism are some of the most essential and burning issues in Europe and all over the world. Some extremely consequential and even fatal judgments and actions – coming from the highest authorities and those holding the greatest power – are formulated in speeches which use the term *multiculturalism*, often undefined and hard to interpret, hard to find out what exactly has been meant by it. Therefore, the task of distinguishing between several different meanings of *multiculturalism* is not just a speculative problem about which academic philosophers can use their privilege to waste time in vain; it has serious ethical and political implications.

The second general goal of this paper is to fulfill the two tasks of discussion in political philosophy, i.e. to contribute to the proper dealing with the issue from two aspects: from normative (the aspect of justice) and from the pragmatic or deliberative point of view. In short: an attempt to found out what is just to do and what is best to do (regarding the problems considered). Beside the already mentioned, other typical philosophical methods are also used, as, for instance, thought experiments.

As the central frame of reference for the following discussion serves the work of the English (and American) scholar Larry Siedentop *Democracy in Europe*.[1] Other relevant components of this frame represent the works of Amartya Sen, Michael Walzer and Joseph Weiler. Every contemporary philosopher who deals with multiculturalism owes a lot to Will Kymlicka. Also in my case, the ideas, arguments and findings of Kymlicka are always on my mind when I am dealing with multiculturalism.

My own general and basic views – which provide the background of all considerations in this paper – can be best described with the terms *solidary personalism*, *liberalism* and *dialogic universalism*.

1.1. Solidary personalism, liberalism, dialogic universalism and secular argumentation in public matters

Solidary personalism can be best understood when compared with nihilism and instrumentalism which form its antipode (Žalec 2011a). Nihilism is a condition of an individual, a group, a society, culture in which on the experiential and intellectual horizons everything is leveled. Nihilistic subject cannot honestly experience one thing or being as more valuable than any other. As nihilism is practically impossible, it usually transforms into some kind of instrumentalism. Instrumentalism is an attitude that

---

[1] Especially Ch. 10 "Europe, Christianity and Islam", in which Siedentop deals with multiculturalism.

does not regard a particular person as a goal, but (at best) just as a means. Contrary to this, for a personalist, every person is always the goal. The main aim of a personalist is flourishing of every person. The problems of nihilism and instrumentalism are the fundamental problems of our age. They seriously hinder or even stop the dialogue, solidarity, approaching other as other etc. All mentioned and to them related goods are essential moments of a personalistic attitude, ethics, relationships and existence. The fundamental (ethical) task (of our age) consists in (finding the ways for) the sufficient and adequate diminishing or limitation of the extent of the instrumentalist reasoning and practice. Deontological ethics is a positive factor of the cultivation of solidary personalism (Žalec 2011a).

The term *liberalism* as used above refers to the philosophical view according to which human freedom represents one of the central values. *Freedom* here denotes the (cap)ability (outer and inner) of a person to live according to his or her reason and conscience.

Dialogic universalism[2] includes the aspiration for universally valid ethics, which however should be developed and established through the dialogue between all concerned parties. There are important universals common to all people that provide the basis on which a consensus about universal ethics can be reached, despite the fact that actual lives of cultures and individuals have their own particularities. The endeavor for experiential and intellectual solidarity is a crucial constituent of dialogic universalism (Hollennbach 2003). Intellectual solidarity is the realization of a genuine dialogue. Dialogic universalism is a reasonable and realistic stance, as there are factual universals of other human conditions. Let's us capture some evidence for the last thesis and reflect on the possibility of pursuing the common global good in the spirit of dialogic universalism by applying the capability approach, pioneered by Amartya Sen and originally philosophically developed by Martha Nussbaum (for more about dialogic universalism and capability approach see Žalec 2008). Dialogic universalism is compatible with and can be supplemented by the belief in the universal common core of the (main) global spiritual and moral traditions, the so called world ethos (Küng 1991), which consists of facets or moments of personalism. Yet, the belief that total intellectual participation in the (intellectual) life of another person is possible – or even striv-

[2] The term was first used by Hollenbach in 1979 (see Hollenbach 2003, 152, n. 23).

ing for it – could be dangerous, because it could mean that we actually do not believe anymore that such a person is transcendent and, hence, we renounce the personalistic attitude towards him or her. We should aim to participate in the lives of the `other` however not at the expense of disrespecting his or her transcendence. The belief that we can totally participate in the experience or life of the 'other' is a dangerous illusion. Solidary personalists always treat themselves and the other as in principle transcendent (Žalec 2011b).

The probably most appropriate attitude towards (cultural) identities might be called – using epistemological terms – critical realism (Žalec 2011b). Neither an attitude that takes the identities as untouchable or overestimates their importance or superiority, nor a stance that diminishes the importance of identity – or even considers it as something that should be destroyed or eliminated because it can only be used for some bad aims, namely to instrumentalize people's attachments, affections, emotions for certain goals (political, economical, etc.) – are proper. Neither a subordination of some individuals to some (collective) identity nor the "nihilistic" attitude about identity, are acceptable. Collective or moral identities are necessary for the individual flourishing, they have their irreplaceable value that should be respected, yet they should also be developable and transformable. The good and acceptable should be accepted and some other elements should be discarded or modified.

The proper stance in liberal democracy toward religion is not outdated, excluding religion from all public life. I think this is clear enough. But some constraints should be set to the religious discourse in the public debate, in particular to what reasons it may be used in public debate on religious issues, especially when certain claims support policy that restrains freedom of citizens. Robert Audi has formulated a set of useful principles, suitable for liberal democracy (Audi 1998). The fundamental and most important of them is the principle of secular rational value, stating that a citizen in liberal democracy has a prima facie obligation not to support any law or public policy restricting human freedom or conduct unless he or she has some adequate secular reason for supporting it. The reason must be adequate from the point of view of public comprehensibility and acceptability (Audi 1998, 160–161).

Will Kymlicka says that there are three stages in the philosophical discussion about multiculturalism: multiculturalism as communitarianism, multiculturalism in the liberal setting, and multiculturalism as a response to the state nation-building. The discussion in this paper will mostly deal with the second stage (Kymlicka 2002).

2. European identity is liberal and of Christian origin

In his well known book *Democracy in Europe* the British scholar Larry Siedentop claims that the European cultural identity[3] is liberal. Identity is the consciousness about which culture is mine and that this culture is specific and particular, being thus distinctively mine. The identity is what binds people together and at the same time distinguishes them from each other. Siedentop further thinks that for the cultivation of the European identity (which is liberal) the narrative must be narrated – to us and to the others – that liberalism is a secular child of Christianity – or its secular twin – and, hence, that the origin of the European identity is Christian.

Siedentop claims that the narrating of this narrative is dangerously jeopardized by two phenomena in Europe: anticlericalism and multiculturalism in the sense of normative leveling of all cultures or opposing to favoring one culture at the expense of others. Let's name such multiculturalism a leveling multiculturalism. Siedentop adds to the above that there is a certain similarity between utilitarianism and leveling multiculturalism: as for a utilitarian all desires are equally valuable, so for leveling multiculturalism are all cultures. Let us immediately add to this some further elucidations about utilitarianism.

On the one hand, the term *utilitarianism* refers to quite different sets of accounts. But still they all share the view that any pleasure is intrinsically good, per se good, in principle good. Otherwise, certain forms of pleasure could be relationally bad, due to their effects or consequences. But if there are no adverse effects or consequences, then any pleasure would be good. So, for instance, the pleasure of Hitler was bad only relationally, because of its implications: Hitler had pleasure, only if millions of people suffered. But if it had been possible that Hitler pleasurable experiences without causing any pain (to others), his feeling of pleasure would have been something good. To illustrate this point, a thought experiment called Nozick's tank could be used (Nozick 1974, 42–45). Nozick's tank is an experience machine in which individuals can make unrealistic, pleasur-

[3] In the text that follows I will use a shorter term *identity* to refer to cultural identity.

able experience, thinking that all their wishes have been fulfilled and that they live the life they desired at most. They live with the illusion of having a perfectly happy life according to their own criteria and wishes. If Hitler had happily lived in Nozick's tank, in illusion that he had ruled the world and that he had killed all the Jews without causing any (adverse) effects in the rest of the universe, then his pleasure would have been something good and he should have been enabled – if only possible – to enjoy it. This is the utilitarian account. It is incompatible with the Christian view. According to Christianity, Hitler's pleasure is intrinsically bad. It is bad as such, regardless of the consequences for the rest of the world, because a man who enjoys such things lives in sin.

In the light of this more precise outline of utilitarianism the Siedentop's thesis about the similarity between leveling multiculturalism and utilitarianism can be more specifically formulated: as utilitarianism claims that any pleasure is intrinsically good, so leveling multiculturalism claims that every culture is intrinsically good. Hitherto, we can set the question: who – if anybody at all – defends such a form of multiculturalism as defined by Siedentop? Is it not rather that such multiculturalism – without any limitations – is only one of the possible accounts which, however, nobody represents? What form of multiculturalism would correspond to Siedentop's specifications and be at the same time real, having actual adherents?

Siedentop remains rather silent about this point. After all, he is a very eminent scientist. His book *Democracy in Europe* was an intellectual bestseller and echoed widely all over Europe. His thesis is quite original and provocative. It carries many interesting implications. The issue of identity and multiculturalism are of crucial importance for the future of Europe and the EU. Out of these reasons, I will try to provide a more elaborate and precise answer to this question. At the same time I will use this opportunity for a somewhat broader presentation of the space of concepts and accounts relating to multiculturalism. And at last, but not least, the outline of this space will enable us to define and station more precisely Siedentop's position and – consequently – better understand its implications.

3. Theoretical space of multiculturalism: concepts and accounts

As first, it should be mentioned that there is a difference between descriptive use of the adjective *multicultural* and the normative discourse about multiculturalism. So, for instance, we may claim that a society is multicultural or some other not, without taking any normative stance in this regard.

To the second group belongs the discourse in which the normative attitude – regarding multiculturality in certain society, situation etc. – is expressed or present. At this normative axis we can discern following normative attitudes towards multiculturality:

1. cultural intolerance;
2. cultural tolerance;
3. cultural accommodation;
4. celebrating of cultural diversity;
5. cultural relativism (Benatar 2008, 219–220).

Which of the above attitudes could be considered as a certain form of multiculturalism? Certainly not the first one, but definitely the fourth one. Whether the second and the third attitude are forms of multiculturalism depends on what kind of positive attitude is needed for a specific attitude to count as multicultural. Is tolerance as such already enough or would something more positive or affirmative be necessary? It is also useful to stress the difference between accommodation and celebration of cultural diversity, as Benatar did (Benatar 2008, 219–220). If merely accommodation is considered, then we are probably only dealing with pragmatics, without any positive valuation of other aspects of multiculturality. The acceptance and positive relationship towards multiculturality can, for instance, originate in the fear from the own consequences of a negative attitude towards multiculturality (Levy 2000). Multiculturality is real, different cultural identities are very important for many people, etc. However, on the basis of multiculturality many harmful phenomena have emerged, but, on the other hand, a negative attitude towards multiculturality had even more adverse effects, as, for example, suppression of some cultures, etc.

From the point of view of cultural relativism, any culture and any cultural praxis is morally acceptable, if actually cultivated by some actual social group (Benatar 2008, 221). Cultural relativism without any limitations is a totally unacceptable position, as, according to it, a very cruel and violent praxis could also be morally acceptable.

Following Siedentop, whose work will to some extent serve as a *fil conducteur* to this paper, I will develop my own views, as I cannot justifiably subscribe to cultural intolerance and even less to cultural relativism. In general, Siedentop – who is a historian of liberalism and a political scientist – rarely explicitly expresses his normative standpoints.

Considering the first three above mentioned points, an additional question appears, which actually could only help to classify the attitudes of individual subjects in one of the three boxes: (in)tolerance towards whom or which cultures? Accommodation of whom or of which specific cultures? Similarly, we can't coherently celebrate cultural diversity without any limitation and, therefore, there is practically no individual who celebrates literally all cultures without any limitation.

Siedentop is certainly in no sense a supporter of celebrating diversity, yet the question is what degree of (in)tolerance and accommodation of cultures he does plead for. How large and of what kind is his (in)tolerance for the presence of different cultures (in Europe) which are not conform with the European liberal culture and do not consequently respect the values of autonomy and individuality or which are even opposing to them? What are the deliberative (pragmatic) and normative (ethical) implications, in case that Siedentop's claims are true? I shall try to answer this question in the following part of my paper. Yet, even before that, I will supplement my description of the theoretical space of multiculturalism and on this ground try to define Siedentop's account and its implications more precisely.

So along the next axis, the following accounts can be discerned in the sphere of multiculturalism (Blum 2008, 193–211):

1. National unity supporting an anti-multiculturalistic account (Schlesinger 1998);

2. The work of Iris Young which established the distinction between class-based inequalities and identity-based inequalities (Young 1990);

3. Liberal culturalism (Kymlicka 1995, 2002; Taylor 1994);

4. Liberal pluralism (Rawls 1993; Galston 2002);

5. Egalitarian criticism of multiculturalism (Barry 2000; Fraser 2003).

Siedentop's account bears some features of the first of the above accounts, which has a negative attitude towards cultural diversity because its adherents think that the plurality of identities corrodes the united national identity which is needed for maintaining of a society or a community.

Siedentop claims that in order to make the EU work, we must narrate the story of the European liberal culture being the child of Christianity. But why is it necessary to do so? Because this narration doesn't tell only that this what is binding us, Europeans, is the liberal culture, but also that this liberal culture has developed from the same origin: from Christianity. Christianity gave birth to what we today underline as the core of the European identity: the liberal culture, respecting the autonomy of every individual. The central components of the liberal culture are of Christian origin. The cradle of respecting the autonomy of every individual is neither antique Greece, nor antique Rome, it is Christianity. This actually implies that the common foundation of the most central beliefs of all Europeans is not liberalism, but Christianity. Liberal culture is only its secular child which latter detached from its parent and even turned in some sense against it. But this detachment from Christianity is in fact not a detachment from the core of Jesus' doctrine and criticizing it is not directed towards this doctrine, but towards the church that is perceived as a bearer of privileges and as an obstacle to progress, emancipation and democratization. Nevertheless, the core elements of mentality with which we, Europeans, identify ourselves as Europeans, or having the European cultural identity, are in essence Christian beliefs with grounding in the Christian faith, metaphysics and theology (Siedentop 2001, 210–211). In order to be able to better understand and formulate the Siedentopian view, I will introduce and explain my understanding of the cultural identity.

Cultural identity consists of psychology, morality, habits and praxis. It also includes certain paradigms, in relation to which the life of the bearers of a specific cultural identity proceeds. The psychological part consists of impulses, (re)presentations, thoughts, valuations and strivings (aspirations). Every morality consists of some values, principles and virtues. Principles and virtues have the function to cultivate and preserve values. Instances of paradigms are Greek temples, Jesus Christ, Bible, Sophocles' King Oedipus, the Constitution, etc. Paradigms are interpretatively inexhaustible and rationally nontotalisable (Dreyfus 2004, 407–419). The interpretations of paradigms and the conflicts of these interpretations are the essential motor and moments of cultural development. Cultural identity includes not only a set of needs but also ways of satisfying of those needs; not only the need for food, family, life partner, etc., but also the way of eating, living a family life or relationship, etc. It includes certain symbols and certain paradigms.

Siedentop claims that there is a special European cultural identity. Its nature is deontological rather than utilitarian because its central value is respecting individual autonomy which also includes respect of his/her conscience. Siedentop claims that the European cultural identity has developed from the Christian cultural identity and that without the latter its development wouldn't be possible. As the Christian identity, the European identity has also two central moments: deontology and respect of individual autonomy. Without them, we cannot speak about the European cultural identity.

The consciousness about belonging to that identity is crucial for the survival of a particular identity. For the cultivation of this consciousness it is crucial to narrate the narrative about the genesis, nature and structure of this identity. Our identity is intelligible, only if grounded on such a narrative, forming an individual with such and such identity. His identity arises from such a narrative. An individual with such and such identity is a moment of such a narrative. If we want that we and the others are conscious who we are, that we and the others understand who we are, understand ourselves, our identity, we must narrate the story about our identity, to ourselves and to the others. However, the cultural identity is not only presented through relevant narratives, it is also established and constructed by it. Without sufficiently wide circulation of appropriate narrative, it can't neither evolve nor survive.

Cultural identity is a way of experiencing the world, but also a way of life in which we are in some sense thrown. The knowledge about this identity, the feeling of it and the consciousness about it, the consciousness that we belong to it, that (many) others have belonged to it and still do, the feeling of solidarity with these others, this knowledge and this feeling are by different bearers of a particular identity of different quality and of different degree. Yet a sufficiently high degree of such feelings and knowledge by a sufficiently large number of people is needed that certain cultural identity actually survives. But – again – this is not possible without relevant narrative and sufficient dissemination of its narrating.

Siedentop claims that there are elements from which we can compose a narrative about the European cultural identity, that actually such a narrative exists. The problem – which jeopardizes the survival of the European cultural identity which in turn is a necessary condition for the EU to work – is that its narrative is not spread widely enough because many wish that it wouldn't be narrated, based on the fact that Christianity plays an important role in this narrative. Many either don't agree that Christianity is of such an importance for the European identity or they don't want to talk about it. Among these opponents – of both kinds – there are two major groups: opponents of the Christian church (anti-clericals) and representatives of a certain form of multiculturalism. The wide range of anti-clericalism and this certain form of multiculturalism in Europe is, therefore, the reason that an adequate narration about the European identity (in Europe) is not narrated and heard enough. The consequence of this is that the European identity (and, thus, the proper functioning of the EU) is endangered.

At this point there are some relevant questions:

1. Why depends a well functioning of the EU so critically on the existence of the European cultural identity?

2. What is the origin of anti-clericalism in Europe?

3. What form of multiculturalism hinders a sufficiently wide dispersion of the relevant narration so necessary for the survival of the European cultural identity?

Let's discuss these questions one after another. I will pay primarily attention – due to the main topic of my paper – to the third question.

4. The meaning of identity in Europe

Let's consider the first question. Siedentop doesn't give an answer explicitly to this question, but it can be derived from some other claims and views from his book.

Siedentop points out that there are two basic types or models of management and arranging of affairs in the European Union: the first is pyramidal and centralistic, the so called 'French model'. The second is a polyphonic system which can be occasionally somewhat chaotic, but which is much more democratic then the first one. It demands, however, a lot of adjustments, reconciliations, dialogues, etc. Pace Siedentop, the consistent implementation of the first model would be fatal for the European Union as it actually renounces the democracy in Europe. Siedentop is, of course, not the only one who has pointed out the dangers of implementing this model in Europe.[4]

Let us return to identity. Why is identity so necessary? We cannot implement the second model in the European Union without the cultivation of a common and living European identity. The first one, the bureaucratic, centralistic, commanding model is the identity of inferior importance. But this model destroys the democracy in Europe. This is already morally unacceptable as such, but beside that, it has also many other unacceptable consequences. Thus, the only way to maintain democracy in Europe is to cultivate a thriving European identity. But this is not possible without a sufficient dissemination of the narrative in which Christianity plays the foundational and fundamental role.

There are some other reputable European scientists and intellectuals that argue in the same direction as Siedentop. One of them is Joseph Weiler. In his book *Christian Europe* he argues that Christianity is the only integral element in Europe (Wiler 2003). Many object to this, arguing that the Enlightenment is (also) an element of integrity. The reply to this objection is twofold: 1. the Enlightenment is not as integrating as Christianity; 2. the Enlightenment is an offshoot of Christianity. Both Weiler and Siedentop agree that Europe doesn't have any other common integral identity apart from the culture which is in its core Christian. They also agree that the dissemination of the truth about Christianity is hindered in

---

[4] Among politicians two, who made themselves very noticeable, could be mentioned. The first is Nigel Paul Farage, a member of EU Parliament (cf. for instance http://www.youtube.com/watch?v=CrPNuHjYTdY (accessed 10. 09. 2012)). The second is Richard Sulik, an economist and a Slovakian politician. Thus, for instance, in the discussion at German TV ARD about the "solidarity" with Greece, he revealed serious problems with democracy in EU, implying that the "French" model is more and more implemented (at the expense of people's money and democracy). Cf. http://www.youtube.com/watch?v=OljfAy-U9pyM&feature=related (accessed 10. 09. 2012). For the Farage's support of the Sulikian ideas in Slovakia cf. http://www.youtube.com/watch?v=PfWKYBR9epI (accessed 10. 09. 2012). For the brief presentation of the process that led to the undemocratic Europe – as it is seen by the critics of EU of the actual situation – cf. http://www.youtube.com/watch?v=O7va2g6kJKg&feature=related (accessed 10. 09. 2012).

Europe. Weiler – himself not a Christian but a religious Jew – speaks about the widespread christophobia in Europe and adds that he has written a book in which he tells the truth about Christianity in Europe, being seriously concerned about the destiny of his own Jewish religion.

5. The origin of anti-clericalism in Europe

A convincing answer to the second question gave Siedentop himself in *Democracy in Europe*. In essence, he claims the following: anti-clericalism in Europe is a consequence of the role and the position of the Christian church in a certain period of the European history. The church acquired several privileges and it has become a part of the ruling class which has hindered the development of freedom and progress. For that reason, many intellectuals who have had in essence Christian values turned away from the church and started to perceive it as a negative factor in society. Such perception has survived until today in a considerable part of the European society and among many intellectuals in Europe. In the USA, the church has never played such a role and therefore, there is no anti-clerical (re)sentiment observed in this form.

6. Which multiculturalism?

It is the high time to consider – in more detail – what forms of multiculturalism really have (or could have) an "anti-Christian" effect, as argued by Siedentop. Siedentop himself doesn't give an answer to this, so I will try to give one.

As mentioned above, there are several forms of multiculturalism. The word *multiculturalism* is a homonym. According to Siedentop, multiculturalism's highest value means preservation of as much different cultures as possible. Such multiculturalism supports everything that contributes to the realization of this value, and refuses all other things. Hence arise some (unpleasant) consequences: the allowance of the suppression of individual freedoms (multiculturalism is a collectivistic attitude) and refusal of any criteria, principles, values etc. which could lead to the reduction of cultural diversity.

So, I cannot agree with the claim that multiculturalism doesn't have any ethical values or criteria in terms of good or bad. It obviously has. Such a criterion is the preservation of the largest possible number of cultures (the largest possible cultural diversity). Multiculturalism applies this criterion also on cultures as such, however refusing those which it perceives as a threat of reducing cultural diversity. Multiculturalism doesn't regard all cultures as equally good or equally bad. But it is true that beside this criterion, it doesn't have any other criteria for the normative judging of cultures.

We should also distinguish between a genuine multiculturalism and actions that can in certain time and circumstances accord to multiculturalism, although they are applied by non-multiculturalists. Such actions are only advantageous to serve their actual purpose. So, for instance, many leftists are not multiculturalists, yet occasionally they support multiculturalism because it serves well their (other) interests.

Multiculturalists hesitate to label some particular culture as particularly important, especially in the case of the dominant or central culture in a particular cultural environment. Thus in Europe they are not willing to stress the Christian origin of the liberal, central and defining moments of the European identity or to speak about these origins.

7. Emotivism and multiculturalism

One of the positive factors of the existence of different forms of multiculturalism in Europe is the wide distribution of emotivist view on morality.[5] According to emotivism, the moral statements are nothing more than expression of our (subjective) emotions, desires, preferences, and interests which however cannot be rationally justified as morally correct or wrong. Emotivists think that moral claims cannot be proved and that they are, therefore, of a subjective nature (or that it is only fair that we treat them as such). No view is morally worse than any other because we don't have any rational criteria for such judgments. [6] Many emotivists, how-

[5] For the detailed consideration of the genesis of emotivism and its place and role in modern society see MacIntyre 2000.

[6] A pragmatic or utilitarian stance often – but not always (Putnam, for instance, argues for a form of pragmatist (Deweyan) position and at the same time refuses expressivism (or non-cognitivism) (cf. Putnam 2008, 377–388)) – goes hand in hand with the refusal of the possibility of rational justification of value statements. This position is called expressivism or non-cognitivism, or emotivism. Richard Rorty was perhaps recently the most famous partisan of it. Accepting of expressivism (combined with a pragmatic or utilitarian attitude) is not only a

ever, agree that the only criterion for refusing certain moral views would be their intolerance toward the 'other' or jeopardizing of the existence of the 'other'. Let's call such emotivists – moderate emotivists.

There is evidently a similarity between emotivism and multiculturalism. On the basis of this similarity, it could be asserted that multiculturalism is in fact a kind of collectivistic emotivism. The essential virtue as of moderate emotivism and multiculturalism is tolerance (except towards the intolerant). The main units of consideration in multiculturalism are whole cultures, i.e. cultural groups, and not individuals; the tolerance in terms of multiculturalism is a tolerance towards other cultures or cultural communities and not a tolerance towards individual as individual. Thus, multiculturalism doesn't need the autonomy of individuals – for justification of tolerance – but it argues in favor of the autonomy of cultural communities. Moreover: multiculturalism denies the autonomy of individuals, if this autonomy jeopardizes the supreme value of multiculturalism. Therefore, we may say that multiculturalism is an instrumental view, because individuals are primarily considered as means for the preservation of cultural diversity. Actually, multiculturalism denies all the rights to individuals when they oppose to the supreme value of multiculturalism. This means that multiculturalism denies also the absolute and universal validity of human rights. Otherwise partisans of multiculturalism quite frequently appeal to human rights, but only in case when they serve to advantage their core values. In the contrary case they are prepared to allow the violation of those rights or even support it. The consequence is that such multiculturalism is in opposition to Christianity, personalism and liberalism. Multiculturalism is similar to emotivism and we may even see it as an expression of emotivism which today to some extent dominates in our Western culture. Yet, multiculturalism is dangerous because it prevents us from getting the correct picture of our identity. But without such a picture we cannot act properly.

---

characteristic of Slovenia or post-communist countries, but also of the dominant mentality in the EU (institutions) in general (cf. Mieth 2008). Siedentop directed our attention to the wide range of economicistic concepts in Europe and the dangers they imply. He claims that economicism has given a posthumous life to Marxism (cf. Siedentop 2001, 164).

8. Pluralist multiculturalism and liberal multiculturalism: Sen's multiculturalism of freedom and choice

I agree with the Sen's thesis from his book *Identity and violence* that freedom of an individual must be preferred to cultural belonging: we must first provide the conditions for the freedom of an individual and then the individual – according to his/her conscience and reason – can decide, what role and place has the culture (from which she/he originates) in his/her life.

I agree with Sen who argues that not all cultures as such are good. According to Anthony Appiah, cultures are not good per se, but rather if they contribute to the autonomy and the flourishing of individuals (Appiah 2005). I think that in cultures we must search for the elements which are in favor such an attitude and support them. Such elements can also help the efforts for global enforcement and implementation of human rights. In order to achieve this goal, it is necessary to link the secular humanists (personalists) and religious humanists (personalists).

Amartya Sen distinguishes between plural multiculturalism and liberal multiculturalism. He refuses plural multiculturalism and argues in favor of the second. Plural multiculturalism claims that the identity of a person is defined with his/her community culture or religion (Sen 2007). It neglects or belittles all other belongings of a person and her/his (social) relation(ship)s, placements, positions, and attitudes (language, (social) class, political views, social roles, etc.). With the habitual preferring of the inherited culture or religion, plural multiculturalism favors the individual's inherited culture or religion to his/her own deliberations and decisions (Sen 2007, 160). Yet, plural multiculturalism in Europe is not something what exists only in somebody's mind as an unlikely possibility, it is reality. As Sen wrote:

"And yet that narrow approach to multiculturalism has assumed a preeminent role in some of the British official policies in recent years.

The state policy of actively promoting new 'faith schools,' freshly devised for Muslim, Hindu and Sikh children (in addition to preexisting Christian ones), which illustrates this approach, is not only educationally problematic, it encourages a fragmentary perception of the demands of living in desegregated Britain. Many of these new institutions are coming up precisely at a time when religious prioritization has been a major source of violence in the world (adding to the history of such violence in Britain itself, including Catholic-Protestant divisions in Northern Ireland – not unconnected themselves with segmented schooling). Prime Minister Blair is certainly right to note that 'there is a very strong sense of ethos and values in those schools.' But education is not just about getting children, even very young ones, immersed in an old, inherited ethos. It is also about helping children to develop the ability to reason about new decisions any grown-up person will have to take. The important goal is not some formulaic 'parity' in relation to old Brits with their old faith schools but what would best enhance the capability of the children to live 'examined lives' as they grow up in an integrated country" (Sen 2007, 160).

There are several important thoughts which should be stressed or reflected on. Such is the opposition to the idea of segregated education[7] which can be a serious obstacle to enabling pupils to be de facto acquainted with other lifestyles (and prepared for them) and with the realization of the Socratic value of the examined life (in favor of which Sen argues). Unexamined life is not worth living, said Socrates. Similarly, we can say regarding freedom: unfree life is not worth living. An individual must be acquainted with the several possible ways of life in order to be able to decide for himself/herself, what kind of life he or she will choose to live. This is the part of respecting an individual as a person.

Sen's ambition is to develop a philosophy and culture of non-violence and peace. He refuses any reductionist division of people according to their nationality, ethnicity, class, religion, and similar. Such reductionism is extremely dangerous also in regard of keeping the peace. As Jeffrey Sachs – one of the reviewers of the book *Identity and Violence* – wrote: "Sen brilliantly shows that when our public policies and attitudes are guided by one-dimensional simplifications of complex societies, we may unwittingly empower the most extreme and least tolerant members of those societies" (Sen 2007, 160). We shouldn't fall to believe that particular one-dimensional identity – which existence is violently defended – is the only one that is good and that solely persons with such an identity can be firm and moral. This is also valid for religious identities.[8]

---

[7] In Slovenia have also appeared such ideas, above all in regard to Roma children.

[8] This danger was very good expressed by Robert Kagan, another reviewer of the Sen's book: "... we need to avoid falling into precisely the trap that Osama Bin

Plural multiculturalism is not compatible with liberalism and hence also not with Siedentopian account presented in this paper. What about liberal multiculturalism? I think that it is compatible. Siedentopian account is not against cultural diversity as such, nor does it claims that only Christianity is good for flourishing of people. It just refuses – like liberal multiculturalism – to sacrifice truthfulness, the freedom of an individual, his autonomy and his flourishing for some other values.

9. Cultural variety or individual freedom

Partisans of cultural variety are inclined to decline individualist premises. They don't see or recognize the need to support the autonomy of an individual because they think that essential differences could be found at the level of culture. The autonomy which they want to protect is that of groups and institutions. They want to protect certain ways of life, and not just some choices of individuals. We are what we are because of the community and culture in which we were raised and not because of some universal and fundamental human nature. Yet – as Trigg points out – if we conclude from such a standpoint that there are no universal ethical criteria which transcend the frames of particular morality of particular groups, then we land in relativism which is incompatible with liberalism (Trigg 2007, 91). The result of such thinking is also a defense of various ways of life inside the same country.

From the liberal perspective, the freedom of choice is of primary importance. For multiculturalists the real freedom is reflected in the existence of different cultures. The first is the evidence for the second. They plead for the autonomy of different ways of life inside the same country. Multiculturalists may insist on that exaggeration by arguing that the freedom of an individual can lead to neglecting of the importance of culture. Some liberally oriented person could strive for the cultural variety based on the

---

Laden has deliberately laid for us: to divide the world into Muslim and non-Muslim (quoted in Sen 2007)". Similar thoughts could be found in the writing of Amanda Heller, another reviewer: "Religion perceived as an absolute identity with no shades of gray I privileged over any and all other human categories and raised as a banner under which not just nations but 'cultures,' equally monolithic, must clash. Drawing on his sophisticated understanding of history and politics as well as economics, Sen reasonably shows such characterizations to be grounded in ignorance of both the past and the present (quoted in Sen 2007)".

belief that a bigger cultural variety offers more possibilities, a larger set of possible choices. Yet a bigger variety of cultures as such doesn't mean at all that an individual has (de facto) more options to choose. As first he/she must have a factual opportunity of choice at all; the autonomy of an individual and her or his choice must be first provided, in order that she or he can chose at all, and if cultural variety is provided at the expense of the autonomy of an individual, the several cultural options it provides are in vain.

Therefore, multiculturalism opens some important and fundamental questions: should the law (and if so, to what extent) protect the rights of individuals or the rights of groups? Should we support the human rights or the rights of groups?

The arguing for the primacy of culture over individuals may originate in care for the maintaining of community. The premise of this thinking is that culture (religion) is what holds community together, what makes community – a community. Culture is that what provides its members with common meanings and on the basis of these meanings they form a community. The cultures are valuable because they are origins of communities which must be maintained.

This argument is defective. Of course, it is true that cultures are essential for communities. But not all communities are good. Is a Nazi community a good community? From the fact that some cultures are indispensable doesn't necessary follow that any culture is good.

10. Paradoxes of multiculturalism

Some forms of multiculturalism claim that nothing remains of the ("non-trivial") self, if we give up our culture (Trigg 2007, 98). But this is not true. The proof is provided already by the claims of many multiculturalists themselves who have put them outside their own (original) culture and they haven't lost their self. Secondly, the mere celebration of cultural diversity implies that we don't take any culture seriously. If all cultures are only a means of cultural variety, why should I truly and sincerely belong to any of them? Nevertheless, multiculturalism itself is actually a form of culture. Multiculturalism is as such dangerous, especially for religions: if there is no difference of value between religions, why should I belong to any religion at all, especially if religion sets inconvenient demands?

Multiculturalism as such is thus a dishonest and inadequate position: at one hand, it looks like suggesting to people that they should remain living inside the frames of their original cultures (how can otherwise these cultures be preserved) and it takes them seriously, yet, at the other hand, multiculturalists themselves don't actually take any culture seriously and basically they step out from their own (original) cultures, they transcendent and embrace the culture of multiculturalism.

I think, contrary to this, that the only coherent and acceptable position is that we honestly admit that for us not all cultures are of equal value, but that we still think that certain tolerance, dialogue, solidarity and also (pragmatic) cooperation between the cultures is needed, out of ethical as well as deliberative or pragmatic reasons.

Secondly, there is no a priori reason that we should celebrate cultural diversity. Cultural diversity is not a proper value, because cultures themselves are just a means for achieving individual freedom and flourishing. We should create conditions in which people are allowed to step out from their original cultures, to link up within new groups and collectives, with new cultures which might be even essentially opposing to their old cultures. To have such freedom is an essential part of respecting of human dignity and personal autonomy. This is one of the main reasons why we should cherish human rights: one of the most important functions and goods of human rights, understood in Western way, i.e. formulated in an individualistic and abstract way, is to allow such disconnections from our original cultures (Žižek 2005, 129). Every human being must be factually enabled to convert, to cut the ties to his/her original culture, to begin a new life, to form new communities, etc. Nothing can be more alien to Christianity as denial of this right. Moreover, honoring it is one of the central moments of Christianity. Just remember Jesus' words that nothing should be prior to us then fulfilling God's will, not even blood relationships (Mr 3:31–35). Yet, this fulfilling is not possible without following and cherishing our conscience, without us being free. For what is a free man, if he is not able to live according to the judgment of his reason and the voice of his conscience?

We may conclude that every form of multiculturalism that opposes this right opposes not only liberalism, but also Jesus' doctrine. Cultural diversity is as a proper, non-instrumental value unacceptable for liberalism, as also for Christianity. It can't be a proper, intrinsic value. But this doesn't mean that we should support any segregation of cultural minorities, that we should deny cultural rights to these minorities[9], that we should not strive for a dialogue and for solidarity with them and among people of different cultures in general, etc. I don't oppose to none of this things, quite to the contrary. All of them are good if they serve to freedom and prosperity of individuals. Moreover, I think that they actually serve and that the so called politics of multiculturalism – for instance in Canada and in Australia – have created many good things and that there are many adverse effects of its absence in Europe – for instance in Germany and in France and in many other European countries. But – at the other hand – we should be aware of the appropriate hierarchy of values. For us, liberals, as Christians and as personalists – no value can be above personal freedom and prosperity. No culture and no cultural diversity. Multiculturalism which opposes to this view should be rejected. But we support multiculturalism in the sense of pleading for the collective cultural rights of minorities, for solidarity and dialogue with them, for integrating them, dialogically and non-violently, into the liberal democratic society. Yet any integration and any accommodation must be accompanied by recognizing differences. We should search for common points among us, but not at the expense of missing to recognize the differences among us.

To achieve coexistence in this globalized and culturally heterogeneous world, where the majority of population will live in big multicultural cities, the sacrifice of some parts of our original cultures will be needed. This doesn't mean that we should not care about maintaining identities of people. On the contrary. Such disrespect would be fatal from the point of view of maintaining peace. Yet, realistically, the "sacrifice" of parts of our cultures is practically unavoidable. This means that the exaggerated celebrating of particular cultures or their moments is even more dangerous than in the past. So is the form of multiculturalism that I reject even more dangerous. Let me, therefore, specify more precisely what an attitude towards parochial, traditionalist or even fundamentalist groups I find appropriate.

---

[9] In Ch. 8 of Kymlicka 2002 the author uses the term *multiculturalism* (and *minority* rights) to denote the demands of ethno cultural groups.

11. Proper attitude of liberal groups toward the traditionalist, parochial or fundamentalist groups

The following question can be raised concerning education and existence or survival of these groups: Do these groups have – in order to secure their existence, survival, or their way of life[10] – a right to educate the pupils in a manner that is unsuitable for a life in liberal democracy or which even shapes the personalities which would oppose it or even undermine it?

I can agree with Michael Walzer that the solution certainly does not lie in abolition of special schools which such communities (already) have (Walzer 2004, 63). What, however, the citizens of liberal democracies must decide upon is which competencies, capabilities, knowledge and virtues the pupils of these schools must develop in order for the democracy to function. Walzer suggests that such requirements should be minimal, although we may cultivate hope that pupils should achieve more. Yet, as he points out, even minimal demands represent a problem for the parochial communities and in no way bring the solution of the problem. There is simply no sound and deciding argument for both parents and authorities to find a way out of the dilemma. Both positions are in some sense justified, yet leave little room for compromising.

There are two extreme possibilities which, of course, are not the only two: first, decay of non-liberal communities, and second, destruction of democracy. Which option should a liberal egalitarian choose? In the situations in which there is a political power at stake we should proceed against authoritarian groups (Walzer 2004, 64). Yet this would be a good solution only in cases of political crisis, but it doesn't bring a solution for everyday situations (Walzer 2004, 65), it doesn't solve the question of coexistence on a daily basis. There is no theoretical deduction from a set of principles for that, only a long, tiresome and unstable succession of compromises.[11]

---

[10] Their Dasein, if we interpret this Heidegger's term as John Haugeland (1995) does, as a way of life.

[11] Those who care for the functioning of a liberal state and liberal democratic society should assent to compromise for good or relevant reasons (cf. Walzer 2004, 65). See also Margalit (2009). We should also not forget that the ability to assent to compromise (for the sake of lesser evil) is an essential part of the virtue

Although the state must tolerate, it does not have the right to impose tolerance on others. As McIntyre correctly points out, local communities are autonomous regarding what to tolerate and what not. This is a decision made by them, as it is also their freedom to draw the line between tolerable and intolerable (MacIntyre 2006, 222).

Toleration is good if it enables us to achieve some individual or common good. The same is valid for intoleration. Toleration must serve to the rational discussion in which also conflicting points may be exchanged, de facto must be, in order to achieve certain goods. But the conflict must be constructive, not destructive regarding achieving of good. Tolerance and intolerance are of service in a constructive conflict.

12. Liberal democracy and policy of recognition and representation of (illiberal) minorities

MacIntyre's ideas sketched above can be applied in creating policy concerning recognition and representation of religious minorities. Herbert has taken an example of a Muslim minority in Europe. Minorities are inheritors of important traditions. As such, they are bearers of morality (values and virtues). So, they should be protected, by adequate recognition and representation. Their protection may include certain autonomy.

But all minorities should not be equally treated. We can follow Kymlicka in distinguishing between three kinds of minorities and three grades of justifiable intervention on the behalf of the state (Kymlicka 1995):

"But he (Kymlicka, n. B. Ž.) does not believe that upholding the primacy of autonomy necessarily entitles liberals to impose their views on illiberal minorities. Rather, he distinguishes between three kinds of illiberal minorities, and grades the degree of intervention that is justifiable accordingly. These groupings are national minorities, such as the Francophone minority of Quebec in Canada; historic minorities such as the Amish in Wisconsin or Hasidic Jews in New York; and recently arrived immigrants, which would include most Muslims in Western Europe. He argues that internal interference should be limited in the first case, cautious in

---

of public reason (or dialogic virtue) which is one of the central civic virtues, i.e. virtues needed for actual functioning of liberal democracies (cf. Kymlicka 2002, Ch. 7). On the liberalism and the politics of lesser evil see Michéa 2009.

the second, but that for the third 'it is more legitimate to compel respect for liberal principles, (…) I do not think it is wrong for liberal states to insist that immigration entails accepting the legitimacy of state enforcement of liberal principles, so long as immigrants know this in advance, and none the less voluntarily choose to come'" (Herbert 2001, 62).

Secondly: Religious minorities should be collectively represented. But this should happen through and be "balanced by a plurality of alternative voices within representative forums, in particular of those who have been historically marginalized within religious traditions" (Herbert 2001, 65). Also in the case of recognition and representation of religious minorities and religious groups in general, we should tend to establish a balance between tradition and political achievements of the modernity: autonomy, equality, and participation. "Thus, if different voices within minority communities can be represented, and a system of individual rights is firmly in place, it seems possible to give greater collective recognition to religious groups without compromising the rights of dissenting minorities within those groups" (Herbert 2001, 63).

13. Tolerance of the non-tolerant

As Walzer suggests, we should tolerate the intolerant but we should deny them political power (Walzer 1990, 80). We should also tolerate minorities and immigrant groups, despite the fact that their ethnic brothers and brothers in faith in other countries are brutally intolerant. As Halik points out, this is the only way that we prove to the intolerant that liberal, democratic and tolerant society is de facto possible (Halik 2009). But to create such a tolerant society, the cooperation between secular humanists (personalists) and religious humanists (personalists) is needed. We must guide our ship between Scylla of fanatic secularism and Charybdis of religious fundamentalism. I may agree with Walzer that we need the separation of state from church, ethnicity and politics (Walzer 1990, 81). Both are needed not only to protect ourselves from fanatic members of religious or other (ethnic, immigrant, political, etc.) groups, but also to protect the non-fanatic, tolerant or democratic members of these groups from their own fundamentalist "brothers and sisters" or co-members. In short: in liberal democracies, we may tolerate the non-tolerant and non-liberal groups, but we must prevent them (also by law) to achieve political power. They may assemble, they may express their opinions, but they shouldn't be allowed to seize the political power.

14. Conclusion

What conclusions can be drown on the assumption that the (Siedentop's) story – about the nature of the European identity, the narrative about it, the role of anti-clericalism and multiculturalism and the meaning of this identity for the future of Europe and the EU – is true?

The first observation is that in Europe we deal with the sacrifice of truth – or with its concealing – about our own identity which means that we conceal (to us) not only the truth about who we are and what binds (or can bind) us together, but also about what distinguishes us from each other. We are dealing not only with the concealing of the truth about us, but also about the others. It is, however, necessary to choose between (speaking) the truth about the Christian origins of our European (liberal) identity on one hand and tolerance, coexistence, cooperation, dialogue, solidarity etc. between different cultures on the other? I don't think so.

The proper Christian faith is not incompatible with cultivation of tolerance and respect for the others.[12] Intolerant Christians have – in this respect at least – moved away from Jesus' way. Christianity has a potential for grounding and cultivation of tolerance and respect for the other. This ground is respect for everybody and this respect is to Christians not only suggested or advised; it is their religious duty (Volf 2011, 12). So, if we support the Christian origin of the European identity, we do not oppose to respecting of other people's culture but rather we ground and justify it as a genuine and truthful European attitude. Therefore, christophobia – based on the care for other non-Christian European cultures (or cultures in Europe) and directed towards genuine Christianity – is groundless. The only thing to be afraid of is misinterpretation of Jesus' teaching as intolerant and disrespectful. But the way to prevent such misinterpretations is not to deny the Christian origins of the European liberal culture. Quite the contrary.

---

[12] For the foundation for such attitude in The Old Testament see Măcelaru 2012. Măcelaru argues that the story of the Tower of Babel (Genesis 11) aims at promoting peaceful cohabitation in spite of cultural differences.

THE CASE OF SLOVENIA FROM THE POINT OF VIEW OF THE THEORY OF CITIZENSHIP

> We carried out our revolution with blood and we cleaned up our house very well during the revolution!
>
> Tito[1]

> [F]or we must – with the experience of the totalitarian century that our people experienced in the whole extent – start again to live with the spirit of the two thousand years old tradition of the gospels and with the praxis of modern, liberal and tolerant community.
>
> Drago Jančar[2]

1. Introduction

In the present text some general ideas and concepts of the theory of citizenship are introduced and presented, and then applied to reflect on the specific situation in Slovenia. The theory of citizenship deals with the praxis and virtues of citizens needed for modern liberal pluralistic democracies to function[3]. Theory classifies those virtues into several groups (cf. Galston 1991; Kymlicka 1995): general virtues which must be respected by every good society (justice, respect of law), economic virtues (like work ethics, abilities to adapt quickly to economic and technological changes), and political virtues. The last group includes the virtues of citizens and the virtues of politicians. For instance, a virtuous politician should not encourage people or give them false hopes across certain limits just to get their support. Moreover, a virtuous politician should not give a promise she/he cannot fulfil (Galson 1991). In this essay three political virtues are taken into consideration: civility, the capacity to object to the centres of power, and the virtue of public reason (Kymlicka 1995).

---

[1] Pirjevec (1995, 156).

[2] Jančar (1998, 23).

[3] For the theory of citizenship and civic virtues see Galston (1991), Kymlicka (1995), MacIntyre (1999), Audi (2000), Flangan & Jupp (2001) and Putnam (1993).

We can notice that in the contemporary Slovenian society the three central civic virtues that we have stressed above are not sufficiently developed and cultivated. In this text we will try to contribute to the understanding of such a condition by taking into account Slovenian history. There are important factors in the (recent) Slovenian history which can help us to understand such a situation. In the essay we particularly focus on the period from 1941 to 1990 (from the beginning of the occupation to the change of regime (from socialist one-party system to liberal democracy)). The Slovenian history from 1941 to 1990 has been characterized by a fratricidal war, violence of the communist authorities and by a totalitarian or authoritarian political system.

2. Civic virtues (in Slovenia)

2.1 Civility

Civility is a kind of political and social decency. Its importance lies in the fact that it is a (maybe the first) bulwark of a non-discriminatory, exclusive or non-solidary society. Hate speech, the mockery of someone due to their physical or mental drawbacks or handicaps, their physical difference (shape of their eyes, colour of their skin, etc.), or their (culturally) conditioned clothes etc. are examples of a violation of this virtue.

Another virtue is the capacity to object to the centres of power. This virtue is vitally important for democracy: just think of the media for instance. It is extremely important to understand the historical reasons for flourishing (or non-flourishing) of this virtue in society. Societies with a totalitarian or authoritarian past have serious difficulties cultivating this virtue, (contemporary) Russia being the most obvious and well-known example.

The lack of civility in Slovenian society can be observed in the example of victims of the communist revolution. Many people speak about bones, not about persons when referring to those killed for being the ideological enemies of communism, and they call people who research the killings bone collectors. Such a discourse has, of course, the function of opening the door to discrimination against the victims as persons. The exclusion of victims from the group of people whose violation of personal dignity must be sanctioned is, of course, a part of rendering the crimes and their persecution unimportant and even evil. The problem in Slovenia is that the majority are – pervaded by the utilitarian ideology of a good emancipative movement and bad anti-modern forces (see the text below) – de facto insensitive for such a violation of decency and civility.

2.2 The capacity to object to centres of power

In Slovenia, the problem of cultivating the virtue of the capacity to object to the centres of power is equally hard as it is in the case of the cultivation of truthfulness and the capacity for dialogue or civility. Important historical factors contribute to this issue (Juhant 2008, Ch. 8). Foreign domination shaped Slovenians into being authority-dependent people. An important role here was also played by the Catholic Church (hereafter CC). The absence of having their own state co-influenced the dependency of Slovenians on the CC and the CC has became the crucial authority for them (Juhant 2008, 154). This historical development has led to a certain ambivalent relationship loaded with tension that has also influenced the subsequent history of Slovenians; under communism Slovenians, who were raised over a long history to be obedient persons, were placed under iron authority. Slovenians were raised for order and assiduity. On the one hand, they are easily (traditionally conditioned) subjected to authority, and on the other hand they exercise their authority exactly as intensely when they themselves are authority. With the communists such a tendency is clearly observable. Slovenian communists were the most obedient executors of orders in communist Yugoslavia. Such historical reasons help us understand the anthropological characteristic of Slovenians: they have little tendency to change the given circumstances, they would rather adapt to them. In such historical conditions, the Catholic faith shaped Slovenians into stable and patient members of society, more inclined to suffering than to aggression. This is manifested even today in the fact that the suicide rate amongst Slovenians is one of the highest in Europe. The communist regime of course suppressed the cultivation of the sense of freedom based on listening to one's own conscience and reason. Instead, it raised people to listen to an all-encompassing ideology which was, however, far from the truth and reality. Instead of using their own reason and conscience, people were stimulated to adapt and to confirm their actions, beliefs, feelings and even imagination to the ideological narrative offered by the authorities. The habit of adapting oneself to the offered ideology rather than listening to your conscience and reasoning based on evidence is naturally not easy to discard. It represents a serious obstacle to the cultivation of critical thinking and hence of freedom in society.

In this regard it is also very important that the CC (and also other churches and religious communities) recognises the importance of acting as a provider of the context which gives sense to the cultivation of the dignity of a person, consisting in the free use of their own reason and conscience, and in acting according to them. The foundation of every free and democratic society can only be an individual who himself/herself is not regarded as an instrument. Rather, he/she is a goal in himself/herself, the main goal is a personal flourishing and freedom of every concrete individual. We can call such a position personalistic[4] liberalism. No church or religion should serve people the truth "on a silver platter" but instead should do everything to ensure that free people themselves pursue the truth. It should resist the temptation of being an all-knowing dictating revealer that de facto does not treat people as persons but in a paternalistic or even instrumental way. It should do all it can to reveal to people the sense of being both truthful and free (in the sense of following their own reason and conscience). That is the only principle foundation of resisting to damaging instrumentalism of which several totalitarian or authoritarian doctrines, economicism or (in the Slovenian case) morally insensitive pragmatic and utilitarian direction today and in the future are only manifestations that can, perhaps more easily than we think, mutate from one form to another. This is the fundamental and the most important mission of the CC and of every church and religious community, including the political dimension of our life.

---

[4] In order to make the following text more understandable, let me shortly explain the meaning of terms instrumentalism, personalism and utilitarianism as I use them. Instrumentalism is an attitude that does not regard some particular persons as a goal, but at best just as a mean to some other goal (domination of the Arian race, reaching of communism). Personalism is an opposite of instrumentalism. For a personalist, every person is always the goal. The main aim of a personalist is the flourishing of every person. The key relevant difference between utilitarianism and personalism is that utilitarianism as such allows for instrumental treatment of particular concrete persons (if this contributes to the increase in total amount of happiness) whereas personalism does not. Calculative manipulation with persons is compatible with utilitarianism, but not with personalism. Thus utilitarianism can function as a foundation or an origin of instrumentalistic attitude. The fatality of the cultivation of a calculative attitude by victims themselves is exemplified by the realization of holocaust (cf. Bauman 1995).

2.3 The virtue of public reason

The virtue of public reason consists of several moments; it is a complex virtue. Its heart represents the capacities for empathy, solidarity, responsibility for the common good, and the capacity for dialogue. Its first important moment is the capacity to articulate our own interests in a publicly understandable way, and to argue for our claims on the basis of publicly relevant reasons. Second, we should not just express our demands and then stop listening to what people say about them and what interests, needs and demands others have in society. In order to actually fulfil this demand, a virtuous person must, from the aspect of the virtue of public reason, be capable of conversation, dialogue and empathy with others. However, even if a strong will and capacity to listen are present and even if there is a dialogue among parties with opposite opinions there are questions in our culturally and morally heterogeneous society about which we cannot reach an agreement. In this case, the capacity to clench our teeth and assent to something even if we do not approve of it in the given situation is the best option (among bad choices). For instance, even if we actually think that every abortion is in fact an act of killing someone, in a given situation we may not support the legal prosecution (potentially with the repressive apparatus of the state) of people carrying out an abortion for we may be aware that in a given situation such coercive measures might bring or actually do bring more evil than good (Kymlicka 1995).

2.3.1 Dialogue

Dialogue constitutes the heart of the virtue of public reason. There are several necessary conditions for any dialogue to take place, the most basic and general being: freedom and equality, openness (absence of taboos), and empathy (Yankelovich 2001). Freedom and equality exclude coercion in dialogue, i.e. the influence of power differences between the participants in dialogue must be sufficiently eliminated. The second condition demands the real possibility be created for every topic and every assumption of the participants in dialogue to be taken into consideration. This implies that no taboos are allowed in real dialogue. Empathy is needed to really 'transfer' our position to the other and vice versa. A good description of empathy including its goal and actual realisation is provided by the concept of intellectual solidarity developed by David Hollenbach (2003). Intellectual solidarity as an attitude is the striving toward my participation in the experience and intellectual life of the other and of an aspiration and endeavour to make the participation of the other part in my experience and intellectual life. True dialogue is the realisation of intellectual solidarity. Freedom of dialogue also demands that we are not obliged to reach any consensus on the topics of disagreement. Of course, there may be a hope that such solidarity will enable a proper solution, agreement, reconciliation and similar to be reached. Yet, all of this should not be understood as an imperative because otherwise dialogue is not free. While there should be no taboos in dialogue, it should not be started with the things that separate us deeply, but with the things that we have in common and that are subject to our agreement. Dialogue is not limited to verbal communication, it is a much deeper way of communication, and a very primitive one (Luckmann 1990). Mediators in conflicts are very well aware of this and one of the initial goals of their strategy is to bring the representatives of conflicting parties to a physically common place where they mutually interact as complete human beings, not just verbally. In a way, this was also stressed by Gadamer and others (cf. Hartmann 2008) when they emphasised the importance of live communication, not just written. Not every communication is already dialogue. Otherwise dialogue would not be such a problem. Dialogue is also not something that can take place, so to say automatically, among people, especially nowadays when people with very different cultural and moral characteristics are brought together and (must) live with one another. On the contrary, the virtue of dialogue is a complex virtue that must be learned and cultivated (Yankelovich 2001).

In addition, there are important factors that jeopardise the realisation of dialogue or even make it impossible. Such an obstacle was the leading prejudice of the former communistic totalitarian regimes, that of the class enemy, that caused hate and exclusion. Its consequences are still present today and bring about mistrust among members of society. The most dangerous obstacles to dialogue are namely hate and mistrust (Yankelovich 2001, 113, 122).[5] They most often originate in violence.

---

[5] For the nature, conditions, factors, kinds and function of trust see Baier (1986), Brewer (1979), Buford (2009) 2009, Fukuyama (1995), Govier (1997), Hardin (2002), Lewis & Weigert (1985), Luhmann (1979), McLeod (2011), Rothstein (2000), Solomon & Flores (2003) and Uslaner (2008).

The degree of generalized trust[6] in Slovenia is very low. The most important negative factors of generalized trust in Slovenia are the following (Žalec 2011d): communist past, low level of truthfulness, the feeling of growing economic inequality (and extremely negative attitude of Slovenians toward it), negative opinion about the work of courts, corruption at high level and lack of (self)responsibility. We should also mention the genocide that has taken place in the recent Slovene history (see the text below). Genocide is an extreme form of mistrust because it means that mistrust to a particular social group is cultivated to such a degree that solely the existence of this group is perceived as a danger that cannot be afforded.[7]

The possibility of expressing criticism in communication is also one of the essential elements of true dialogue. Dialogue is impossible without critical thinking. But for dialogue to be really possible – without causing destructive effects that could result in ruining dialogue – the principle of discerning someone from his/her convictions and acts is de facto necessary. In the opposite case of identifying persons by their beliefs and deeds, we are actually telling those persons that they are bad, and not only that their deeds or attitudes are bad.[8]

---

[6] For the explanation of this concept see Uslaner (2008).

[7] See Chirot & McCauley (2006). For the sociological and legal aspects of Slovenia as a democratic state governed by the rule of law see Igličar (2011). The research of public opinion from 2004 showed that Slovenians trusted less their legal system than citizens of France, Germany, Canada and USA in the comparable period. The research of public opinion in 2011 showed that the degree of trust of Slovenians in court, state administration, prime minister, government, parliament and political parties is rather low. The mentioned institutions are ranked in the stated order (from the top to the bottom). The trust in courts equals the trust in clergy. At the top we find firemen. (Cf. Igličar 2011, 66–67) For the violation of human rights and basic liberties in Slovenia from 1945 to 1990 see Šturm (1998). Communists in Slovenia (in that period) faithfully followed Krylenko's command that court is an organ of the class-struggle of workers against their enemies (see Simoniti 1998).

[8] We should treat people in the spirit of love towards a man and hate towards his incompleteness, weakness, vices, "sins". As St. Augustine wrote: « Et hoc quod dixi de oculo non figendo, etiam in caeteris inveniendis, prohibendis, indicandis, convincendis, vindicandisque peccatis diligenter observetur, cum dilectione

The virtue of public reason is especially important for developing deliberative democracy, as opposed to aggregate democracy (Kymlicka 2000). The development of democracy according to the deliberative model is particularly important for the stability of democracy and society in general. Such a democracy presupposes that issues (of controversy) are debated among the opposite parties, that people are acquainted with several views and with a broader set of possible consequences of their decisions. So responsibility is clearer, disappointments are reduced etc., which contributes to a more transparent, more democratic and freer directing of society, and of course to its stability. It is exactly this last value that is of great importance in modern times of instability, and therefore the carrying out of deliberative democracy should be one of our central aims which of course presupposes the cultivating of the virtue of public reason in society.

3. Origins of violence: the importance of solidarity

Tolerance and the culture appropriate for a modern pluralistic and value heterogeneous society are seriously endangered by violence. Following Gandhi and Sen, we may say that the reduction of violence as much as possible is a reasonable value that every healthy society should strive for (Sen 1997). Accordingly, we should ask ourselves about the nature of society that hinders or stimulates violence. We consider the following characteristics to be crucial: personalism, inclusion and solidarity.

The opposite of inclusion is marginalisation. Marginalisation causes violence which, in turn, threatens stability and democracy in society. Inclusion means solidarity, material, intellectual and other, that means our sharing of intellectual life and of other goods in society, participation in the common good of society. The extreme case of exclusion is, for instance, a violation of human rights (like in concentration camps) and for this reason Hollenbach (2003) understands human rights as an institutionalisation of human solidarity. A personalist society is society in which the dignity of persons is respected. The development of the capabilities of persons to freely use their reason (the capacity to know) and their conscience is supported and cultivated in personalist societies. Our thesis is

---

hominum et odio vitiorum « (*Epistola* 211, par. 11). See also *Regula ad servos Dei*, 4, 28 (St. Augustine 2011).

that a negative factor of violence is solidarity and that violence often originates in a lack of solidarity. What is the evidence supporting this thesis? It can be found at several levels: from neurological through psychoanalytical to psycho-historical.

Neurological evidence is provided by modern cognitive science. Joachim Bauer reports on this matter (Bauer 2006). For instance, he reports on a special substance called dopamine which our body secretes when we are in good relations with other beings, when we are included in a human group and similar. The secretion of dopamine brings about good mood and it is a kind of a natural drug we are addicted to. In the case of being excluded, we experience some sort of an abstinent crisis and it is possible to search for a dopamine surrogate in inappropriate ways, for instance by using synthetic drugs, going to a prostitute etc. This supports the flourishing of criminal business which in turn brings violence into society and generally endangers the whole society. Margot Sunderland (2006) directs us to the importance of a proper loving relationship with our children in order to avoid the very damaging bio-chemical state of a baby's brain which can be permanent. The systems of vital importance, connected with the chemical substances that have effects on emotions, like opioids, noradrenalines, dopamine and serotonin—these systems are still developing in undeveloped brains—might be seriously damaged and might cause a chemical non-equilibrium in a brain. Sunderland, for example, claims that a low level of serotonin is one of the key factors of depression and also of violent behaviour (2006). Serotonin, a chemical substance in the brain is a very important factor for social and emotional intelligence. An optimal level of serotonin might stabilise one's mood, diminish aggressiveness and for that reason plays an important role in the strengthening of good relations. Researchers have shown that monkeys that were very respected in their society and were at the top of the social hierarchy had the optimal level of serotonin. The level of serotonin is strongly influenced by human relations, either positively or negatively. Researchers have proven that stress in early life might influence the system of serotonin in the developing brain of a little child in a damaging way. On the contrary, the loving moments you share with your child positively influence the level of serotonin in the ventromedial cortex. If a child shares many beautiful moments with you, they will get used to the optimal level of serotonin in their brain and that will become a part of their true personality. A low level of serotonin in animals and humans is connected with their impulsive behaviour. Serotonin, a chemical substance which equilibrates one's mood, in that case cannot calm the emotional reactions of a man or an animal down. When such a person or an animal gets angry, we are not just dealing with a mild form of irritation or reluctance but with a mad, horrible fury. It is well known that monkeys with a low level of serotonin are impulsive and aggressive (Sunderland 2006, 223). That should be enough about the neurological reasons. We think the message is clear enough.

The findings of psychoanalysis point in the same direction. The phenomena that psychoanalysis describes as identification with the aggressor, the protective mechanism of projection and projective identification, and the protective mechanism of splitting (Bohak 2008) should be mentioned here. In the first case, collectives that are themselves victims of violence consequentially carry out similar violence on other collectives. As far as the last phenomenon is concerned, we deal with people whose parents did not respond to their needs or offer them their attentiveness, care or love in their childhood. Such an attitude causes the development of a negative self-image in their children. The complex in which the negative self-image is interwoven with a twofold relationship with the parents (on the one hand such people usually speak about a kind-hearted daddy and mummy, but on the other hand, they perceive them as monsters, they hate them) results in violence towards other people. Psychotherapists are familiar with the fact that violent patterns of behaviour are transmitted from one generation to another (many victims of violence in their later life themselves search for a violent environment) if proper treatment does not break the cycle of transmission. Last but not least, the aggression someone directs towards themselves should also be considered, namely suicide.

In his essay about trauma and suicide among aborigines at the North Pole and in Australia, Antoon A. Leenaars (2005) hypothesises that a similar phenomenon as in Australia and at the North Pole also took place in Lithuania under the Soviet occupation. The characteristic of aboriginal societies is that before the colonial occupation the suicide rate among the population was not high. The same is true of Lithuania. Today, all these societies are burdened by suicides as if they were an epidemic. In the case of aboriginal societies the rate of suicide is five times higher than among the white population. According to Canadian researchers the causes of such suicides among Inuits are: poverty, divorce, and loss of children, accessibility of firearms, alcoholism, personal and family health problems, past sexual and bodily abuses. But Leenaars thinks these phenomena are the effects of genocide.

The arrival of colonialists was—from the point of view of aborigines—a threat of destruction to aboriginal world, culture and, last but not least, of extermination of aboriginal people. Colonialists were prepared to exterminate aboriginal people. As Leenaars points out something similar might be said about Soviet occupation of Lithuania. Soviets wanted to assimilate Lithuanians and thus to destroy their previous world and culture. Similar things happened in Slovenia after communists took power in 1945. We witnessed a radical attempt to destroy the traditional, catholic, bourgeois and rustic world and culture in Slovenia (Dežman 2008, 372ff).

One might object that in the case of Slovenia we cannot talk about genocide if we accept the UN *Convention on the Prevention and Punishment of the Crime of Genocide* from 1948.[9] This convention limits genocide to the intention to destroy a national, ethnic, racial or religious group. However, the definition of genocide from UN convention is not adequate. We can consent to Leo Kuper (1981, cf. Jones 2011, 16–17) that this definition is not good and that its main drawback is that it leaves out the political groups from the list of groups it protects[10]. In modern world the political differences are at least equally important—as a foundation for mass killings and destruction—as racial, national, ethnic or religious differences. Thus, Chirot and McCauley (2006) claim that the greatest genocides of the 20th century were ideological, not ethnical. Besides, the genocides of racial, national, ethnic or religious groups are the consequence of political conflicts or they are connected with them. Despite critical remarks, Kuper thinks that it is not good to change the meaning of the expression which is internationally accepted. Yet, on the other hand such a use of the expression genocide renders an adequate consideration of "genocides" committed over groups not covered by the definition of

---

[9] Accessible at http://www.preventgenocide.org/law/convention/text.htm (May 4th, 2011).

[10] The deficiency that political, economic and cultural groups are not alleged in UN convention is partly repaired by the *Convention for the Protection of Human Rights and Fundamental Freedoms* (Rome, November 4th 1950, accessible at http://www.media-forum.si/slo/pravo/pravni-viri/evropska-konvencija.pdf (May 4th, 2011)).

UN convention impossible. For this reason, Kuper uses expressions like liquidating or exterminating acts. This solution seems to us rather ill-fated because these expressions are too loose. Thus, I keep the word genocide but I use it as referring also to crimes over political groups and classes. I use the word genocide for any intentional destruction of persons solely on virtue of their (factual or just ascribed) belonging to a particular group. It follows that there can be many kinds of genocide. In scientific literature we can find a set of many different terms (Jones 2011, 26ff): classicide, democide, ecocide, eliticide, ethnocide, femicide/feminicide, fratricide, gendercide, judeocide, linguicide, memoricide, omnicide, politicide, poorcide, urbicide.

For the mass killings in Slovenia in spring 1945, we may use the terms classicide (a term coined by Mann (2005, 26)) and politicide[11] (an expression introduced by Harff and Gurr (2003)). Classicide is an intentional mass killing, liquidation or destroying of people on the basis of their belonging to a particular social class. Politicide is destroying of people on the basis of their belonging to a particular political group. Barbara Harff and Ted Gurr maintain that revolutionary one-party states are the most often perpetrators of politicide (Jones 2011, 28).

If we add to the above evidence the numerous examples showing, almost as a rule, that violent persons and collectives were themselves subjected to violence, we may conclude that the violation of solidarity is the fundamental source of violence in society.

4. The Slovenian case

Slovenia (currently with about 2 million citizens) is the only member state of the EU that has itself experienced (as a victim and as a perpetrator) all three forms of "totalitarianism"[12]: fascism, Nazism and communism. Perhaps only the Greek experience can be seen as comparable up to a certain degree (Dežman 2008, 258, n.13). The most important of them—also for the present situation—is communism in its Titoistic ver-

---

[11] Pučnik (1998, 40) also characterizes mass killings in Slovenia after the war – carried out by the state – as genocide.

[12] The term totalitarianism is here used in quatation marks because I don't classify fascism as totalitarianism yet in the Slovenian context the talk about these regimes as three totalitarianisms is quite common.

sion. A *Kulturkampf* took place in Slovenia already in the 19th century among anti-modern Catholics and liberals, but it reached its culmination and actually transcended the scope of this concept (becoming a fratricidal war between the sides directed by the communist and anti-communist sides (mostly Catholics)) during the WWII and immediately after it.

Slovenia was maybe the biggest mass scaffold and graveyard in Europe after the end of the Second World War (Dežman 2008). More than 600 hidden mass graves are scattered all around Slovenia (cf. Ferenc 2012, 238). In such murders without any court process immediately after the Second World War thousands of Slovenians were killed. What are the exact numbers of the killed? The leading Slovenian expert for the hidden mass graves in Slovenia has written:

> The exact number of victims lying in secret graves will probably never be known. The Republic of Slovenia has in the past few years succeeded in preparing a name-list of all residents of Slovenia who died a violent death in the Second World War and immediately after. Judging by the available data, around 15 % – that is around 13.960 (of those 12.587 Home guards, 160 Slovene Chetniks, and 1.127 civilians) – of about 84.000 people who died by January 1946 were individuals killed after the war ended (Čepič, Borak & Fischer 2005, 790–795). Trying to answer the question of how many Croats and people of other nationalities were killed in Slovenia and where their remains could be found is even more difficult. As there is almost no primary archive material about the killings, mass graves or the number of victims as well as due to very rare excavations of the posthumous remains, to estimate or even to determine such a number could all too soon become a subject to manipulation and reach unprecedented levels (Ferenc 2012, 233).

The goal of the communists in Slovenia and the whole of Yugoslavia (Bajt 2007) was of course revolution, to which all their activity was subordinated, and their main goal was not fighting the occupation forces but destroying the ideological (class) enemy. To support this thesis: the number of occupation forces killed in Slovenia by Slovenian partisans was only around 5.000 which is just a fifth of the Slovenian victims who were killed for being an ideological enemy (Dežman 2008, 284).

Data that we find in the works of some other Slovenian historians allow the following approximate representation:

Table 1: Victims among Slovenians (Dežman 2008, Granda 2008)

Slovenian population in 1941	1.500.000	100 %
	Number of victims	Percentage of whole population
Victims of the fratricidal war	30.000	2 %
Victims killed by partisans or communists	25.000	1,7 %
Victims killed by partisans or communists after the war	18.000	1,2 %
Victims killed by anti-communist side	4.000	0,3 %
Political emigrants after the war	7.000	0,5 %

The logic of Titoism is pretty simple: everything that serves the revolution is good, everything that opposes or hinders it must be eliminated, even with intense violence. However, the question remains why the revolution captured Slovenia to such a high degree. Titoism was sustaining itself through permanent crises and purges. The indulgences to liberalism only served to strengthen the power of the particular rule of individuals or groups. Tito's competencies in the 1974 Yugoslav Constitution are only comparable with the powers of Hitler, Stalin. Tito did not settle the question of his successor, either. Such a structure of power, which was only a front for the political reality, meant that the extremely difficult future of Yugoslavia was predictable (Dežman 2008, 262). Silvin Eiletz (2008) proved that purges were the centre of life in the Yugoslav communist party from its beginning. Tito accepted the Stalinist model of mutual reckonings inside the party and succeeded to survive it as a winner. His years in Moscow are surely an important origin of the subsequent homicides Tito is mainly responsible for. In the Moscow years Josip Broz-Valter (later Tito) hardened. He was shaped by fear and horror. Further, Tito's team was also educated in Moscow (the Slovenian top communists Kardelj, Kidrič, Bebler were important parts of the Yugoslav Party leadership) and involved in the same hardening system. The Slovenian circle around Tito implemented the Stalinist model in Slovenia without mercy. This is a part of the answer why in just one year an important share of Slovenian people became wild and criminal even though there are no historical premises to explain such a development. Up until 1941 Slovenians were "normal" people and every crime was prosecuted by the police. One year later and this small nation was captured by a storm of crime, and after 1945 this crime was not prosecuted by the police but became legal (Dežman 2008, 265–266; Juhant 2008, 153–206).

How was that possible? Some important facts must be noted in this regard: communist leaders educated in Moscow came back to Slovenia; the secret police (OZNA (UDBA)) was established[13]; communist leaders (partly educated in Moscow, partly by partisans, partly in post-war Yugoslavia) quickly started with prosecutions, torture and killings. The transition from "normality" to "wildness" is then accountable by means of mass psychology[14]. In the end, the process of the ideological transformation of Slovenian society evolved into a state in which broad layers of the nation, many of them wilfully, supported the authoritarian socialist system and were associated with numerous political organisations. Ultimately, communism in Slovenia was not some dictatorship of the minority above the majority: the majority supported the regime and sympathised with it. After the fall of communism, people with blood on their hands integrated into the democratic system, appearing as if they were incapable of committing such crimes at all (Dežman 2008, 266).

In this brief overview of the recent history of Slovenia we should say that those who suffered were not only the killed persons themselves, but also their relatives (widows, children, *etc.*). They were subjected to horrible torture, discrimination and humiliation. Children were robbed of the love of their parents. Such victims numbered between 150.000 and 200.000 people (Dežman 2008, 266).

In 1990, a plebiscite about secession of Slovenia from Yugoslavia was carried out in Slovenia: an attendance level of 93.2%, and a 95% affirmative answer. In 1991, Slovenia declared its independence and officially became a liberal democracy. Its *Constitution* defines it as a democratic

---

[13] Hannah Arendt (1962) pointed out that the characteristic of totalitarian regimes is a very high rank of secret police. Above it is only the leader.

[14] For such an account, see Dežman (2008, 266–269). Dežman concludes: "When the conditions were given for the development of killing personality and the production of hatred other as the ideological-political product started, the transition from boys who attended religious education and mass to serial murderers was possible" (269).

state governed by the rule of law and as a social state. In 2004, Slovenia joined NATO and the EU, while in 2007 it introduced the euro currency (becoming the first post-communist country to do so).

The CC was under pressure already during the war and especially after it. It is true that some of the clergy supported the anti-revolution, but only some members of the Ljubljana's diocese. But after the war the communists also imprisoned clerics from the province of Primorska who had fought against fascism, and clerics who during the war had been banished from the provinces of Styria (Štajerska) and Upper Carniola (Gorenjska). Many clerics were tortured or killed (in unexplained circumstances). From 1945 to 1961, of around 1.000 clerics 429 went before the court, 339 were punished with imprisonment, 73 financially and 9 were sentenced to death (4 of these sentences were actually carried out). The communist authority tried to break the Church down by all means: physically, ideologically and of course economically. Although the communist regime in Yugoslavia was later more indulgent in the field of domestic policy, special departments inside the secret political police were never dismissed. The communist authorities tried to organise the anti-Catholic Church, and of course also sought to split the CC internally and deepen the discord with the Protestant and Orthodox churches. After the war, some Protestant clerics were also persecuted, along with some members of smaller religious groups like Jehovah's witnesses (Granda 2008, 235; Juhant 2008, 165–176).

Table 2: Victims among clerics in Slovenia from 1945 to 1961 (Granda 2008)

Number of all clerics in Slovenia	1000	100 %
	Number of victims	Percentage of whole number of clerics
Clerics that went before the court	429	42.9 %
Punished by imprisonment	339	33.9 %
Financially punished	73	7.3 %
Sentenced to death	9	0.9 %
Death sentence actually carried out	4	0.4 %

Yet, despite all of this, things slowly started to settle down. In 1961 the Ljubljana diocese was established, in 1968 the Ljubljana metropolis was set up (the Maribor diocese was subordinated to it). According to the Osimo agreements from 1977 (signed by Italy and Yugoslavia), the question of the Koper diocese was finally settled and it was included in the Ljubljana metropolis. In the framework of the Yugoslav bishops' conference, the Slovenian provincial bishops' conference was established which in 1992 formally seceded from the Yugoslav one. In 2006, three new dioceses were established: Celje, Murska Sobota and Novo mesto. The first two form part of the Maribor archdiocese, while the third one belongs to Ljubljana. The Vatican recognised Slovenia as an independent state in January 1992, confirming the efforts of the Slovenian Catholic Church which had actively participated in efforts for independence. Pope John Paul II visited Slovenia twice, in 1996 and 1999 (Granda 2009, 235).[15]

The magnificent result at the plebiscite indirectly made lustration impossible (Juhant 2008, 180–183). It could not have been carried out completely, but at least those responsible for the most horrible crimes after the war could have been justly punished. Instead, no person was put on trial, not to mention being sentenced. The dull reckoning with the totalitarian past is a huge problem for Slovenia. In any case, the political polarisation (that sprung up during the independence process)—the separation between new parties and those arising from the old communist party and its successors—is one of the characteristics of Slovenia's political reality. The past also strongly separates Slovenians in present times (Granda 2008, 257).

A huge number of people in Slovenia were deprived of any solidarity (intellectual or material), were excluded (for instance a violation of their human rights, which is an extreme form of exclusion) and their personal dignity was not respected etc. This group constitutes the unarmed victims of the war and post-war killings and their relatives (widows, children etc.). The level and content of private and public discussion in Slovenian society indicates that today an important section of Slovenian society does not show any solidarity or true compassion to these victims. They do not see it as an injustice that their unjust suffering is not justly recognised or responded to. A kind of utilitarian and pragmatic ideology is preferred

[15] About the situation of the CC in Slovenia after the Second World War see also Dolinar (1998) and Griesser-Pečar (1998).

to justice and a moral stance[16]. Many people do not care at all whether the crimes will ever be sanctioned and the suffering at least partly ameliorated. Interest in the truth and morality is totally absent as regards victims from the Catholic side. On the other hand, a lot of hostility is present against the CC. These two phenomena are interrelated. In an important part of Slovenian society the CC is perceived as greedy, hypocritical and a threat to freedom. The mentioned victims are also perceived as a necessary cost in the process of emancipation from fascist and clerical "totalitarianism". Some critics of the CC speak about the fourth totalitarianism, namely the clerical totalitarianism of the CC, and warn that the aim of the CC is to take the place of the communist party in society (cf. Hribar 2004), even though according to empirical data on the religiously relevant attitudes of Slovenians that seems incredible. Many people support the exclusion of people who speak about the killings because they perceive them as endangering free society and the achievements of the modern emancipative movement in fighting anti-modern forces, and as just using the victims for their own anti-emancipative and anti-modern goals. These views are widespread among ordinary people but, of course, they also have representatives among the theoretical elite (cf. e.g. Luthar & Luthar 2003).

Another closely related attitude is that we must speak about victims, that we must respect the dead etc. Yet the fratricide war is understood simply as a war between two totalitarian streams: communist and clerical; and

---

[16] The quantitative research of Niko Toš and group provides some empirical evidence for our thesis (see Toš et al. 1990): "In the year 1945 Yugoslav and Slovene communist authorities secretly killed – in Rog and other places – thousands of the members of Home guard and other refugees that Englishmen sent back from Austria to Slovenia. Choose the answer that best expresses your view on those killings! How would you then characterize those events?", the following responses were given by the citizens: 1. As a horrible crime 48.0%.; 2. As a big political mistake 19.5%; 3. As understandable act of revenge 6.6%; 4. As a tragic yet unavoidable consequence of the civil war 11.5%; 5. As a punishment for betrayal of own nation 8.0%; 6. I don't know 6.5%. The research shows that less than half of Slovenes thought that mass killings of refugees in Slovenia were a crime. All other do not think that somebody should be morally condemned or sentenced for it. The level and content of private and public discussion in Slovene society indicates that the public opinion has not importantly changed till today.

the responsibility for such a mentality of the Slovenian communists is shifted to the side of the CC as Slovenian communists are described as having been mentally shaped by the CC and are therefore a mirror image of the CC's totalitarian mentality (cf. Hribar 2004). But the actual political impact of this attitude is that we should symbolically[17] respect the dead people, but politically keep fighting against the CC as the most dangerous agent in modern Slovenian society.

Such an atmosphere of anti-CC sentiment perceives the CC as a greedy and power-seeking institution that threatens the freedom and achievements of emancipative movements (which had their erroneous deviations or movements, but now this is the past) which makes any solidarity with the victims of communism impossible. On the other hand, such a non-personalist and pragmatic or utilitarian stance toward victims of communism can be seen as a transformed survivor of what is in a sense an instrumentalist ethics of communism[18].

The period from 1941 to 1990 in Slovenia was marked by strong and widely spread presence of fear, violence, silence about the crimes of the communist regime and non-solidarity with its victims (cf. Jančar 1998, 11–23; Simoniti 1998). All this was accompanied by very aggressive

[17] In any case, only symbolic gestures are not enough. As Ferenc has insisted, beside symbolic acts we must support and carry out also concrete research and actions that exactly reveal and document factual truth about Slovenian past (cf. Ferenc 2012, 238). Pučnik (1998, 47–48) pointed out that the popular tactics of people who want to prevent the revealing of truth was the supporting of symbolic gestures, erecting of abstract symbolic monuments and setting signs on the one hand and hindering of carrying out of concrete and determinate researches, collecting concrete data, making exact lists and catalogues etc. on the other.

[18] A pragmatic or utilitarian stance often, but not always (Putnam (2008) for instance argues for a kind of pragmatistic (Deweyan) position and at the same time refuses expressivism (or non-cognitivism), goes hand in hand with the refusal of the possibility of rational justification of value statements. This position is called expressivism or non-cognitivism, also emotivism. Richard Rorty was perhaps the most famous recent partisan of it. Accepting of expressivism (combined with a pragmatic or utilitarian attitude) is not only a characteristic of Slovenia or post-communist countries but also of the dominant mentality in the EU (institutions) in general (cf. Mieth 2008). Larry Siedentop (2000) directed our attention to the wide range of economicistic thinking in Europe and its dangers. He wrote that economicism has given a posthumous life to Marxism.

propaganda which pictured the opposite side as the embodiment of evil and inhumanity. According to the instrumentalist doctrine that Slovenian communists accepted, particularly two social "elements" were considered as especially dangerous class enemies that deserve regardless treatment: the so called "burgeois right" and the Catholic Church (Simoniti 1998, 35). Apart from them, farmers were also considered as "natural" enemies of communism (cf. Dežman 2008).

5. Conclusion

Violence and fear are two main and fundamental negative factors of dialogue. Dialogue is the heart of the virtue of public reason. Hostile propaganda that we witnessed in Slovenia during the war and in the time of the communist power is an extreme form of non-civility. Fear, non-solidarity and a habit of silence are the best ground for the absence of capacity to object to the centers of power.

In the period of the totalitarian or authoritarian system in Slovenia, the central civic virtues were almost completely absent: civility in regard to those who were perceived as the enemies of the regime, a capacity to object to the centers of power and the virtue of public reason which is essentially constituted by dialogue. Solidarity with the victims of the communist regime was absent too. An insufficient cultivation of the mentioned virtues is also a characteristic of the present Slovenian society. Such a situation is in a large part due to the "ice berg of the past that still wants to rule over us" (Jančar 1998, 383-386).

Culture consists of habits that change very slowly (Fukuyama 1995). In Slovenian (political) culture there are strongly present sediments of the past that mutilate development and cultivation of civic virtues in Slovenia.[19]

[19] My thanks go to Janez Kolenc and Vojko Strahovnik for their valuable suggestions and comments to the drafts of this text.

REFERENCES

Appiah, K. A. 2005. *The Ethics of Identity*. Princeton, N.J.: Princeton University Press.

Arendt, Hannah. 1962. *Origins of Totalitarianism*, London: Allen & Unwin.

Audi, Robert. 1998. A Liberal Theory of Civic Virtue, *Social Philosophy & Policy*, Vol. 15, 1, pp. 149–170.

Audi, Robert. 2000. *Religious Commitment and Secular Reason.* Cambridge: Cambridge University Press.

Baier, Annette. 1986. Trust and Antitrust. *Ethics*, Vol. 96, No. 2, 1986, pp. 231–260.

Bajt, Drago. 2007. Nesmiselnost partizanskega osvobodilnega boja (Absurdity of the partisan liberating struggle). An interview given to B. Nežmah. In: B. Nežmah, *Zrcala komunizma: intervjuji 1994–2005* (*Mirrors of communism: interviews 1994–2005*), Ljubljana: Modrijan, pp. 35–47.

Barry, Brian. 2000. *Culture and Equality: An Egalitarian Critique of Multiculturalism*. Cambridge: Polity.

Bassiouni, Cherif. 2003. Zločini protiv čovečnosti (Crimes against humanity). In: Roy Guttman & David Reif, *Leksikon ratnih zločina: Ono što bi javnost trebala da zna* (trans. by N. Novović & M. Marjanov, orig. *Crimes of War. What the Public Should Know* (1999)). Beograd: Samizdat B92, pp. 535–537.

Bauer, Joachim. 2006. *Prinzip Menschlichkeit: Warum wir von Natur aus kooperieren*, Hamburg: Hoffmann und Campe Verlag.

Bauman, Zygmunt. 1995. *Modernity and the Holocaust*, Cambridge: Polity Press.

Bellinger, Charles K. 1992. Toward a Kierkegaardian Understanding of Hitler, Stalin, and the Cold War. In: George B. Connell and C. Stephen Evans (eds.), *Foundations of Kierkegaard's Vision of Community: Relig-*

ion, Ethics, and Politics in Kierkegaard. New Jersey: Humanities Press, pp. 218–230. Reprinted in Bellinger 2010.

Bellinger, Charles K. 2001. *The Genealogy of Violence: Reflection on Creation, Freedom and Evil*. New York: Oxford University Press.

Bellinger, Charles K. 2008. *The Trinitarian Self: The Key to the Puzzle of Violence*. Eugene, OR: Wipf & Stock Pub.

Bellinger, Charles K. 2010. *The Joker Is Satan and So Are We: And Other Essays on Violence and Christian Faith*. CreateSpace Independent Publishing Platform.

Benatar, David. 2008. Diversity Limited. In Thomas, L. (ed.), *Contemporary Debates in Social Philosophy*. Malden: Blackwell, pp. 212–225.

Beznec, Barbara (ed.). 2007. *Zgodba nekega izbrisa* (*The story of some erasure*). *Časopis za kritiko znanosti, domišljijo in novo antropologijo*, Year 35, No. 228.

Blum, Lawrence. 2008. Ethnicity, Disunity, and Equality. In Thomas, L. (ed.), *Contemporary Debates in Social Philosophy*. Malden: Blackwell, pp. 193–211.

Bohak, Janko. 2008. Religija in nasilje – psihoanalitski pristop (Religion and violence – a psychoanalytical approach). *Znamenja*, 38, 3–4, pp. 35–48.

Brewer, M. B. 1979. In-Group Bias in the Minimal Intergroup Situation: A Cognitive Motivational Analysis. *Psychological Bulletin*, Vol. 86, No. 2, 1979, pp. 307–324.

Buford, T. O. 2009. *Trust, Our Second Nature: Crisis, Reconciliation and the Personal*. Plymouth: Lexington Books.

Card, Claudia. 2010. *Confronting Evils. Terrorism, Torture, Genocide*. Kindle Edition.

Chirot, Daniel & McCauley, Clark. 2006. *Why Not Kill Them All? The Logic and Prevention of Mass Political Murder*. Princeton and Oxford: Princeton University Press.

Cohen, Roger. 2003. Etničko čišćenje (Ethnical cleansing). In: Roy Guttman & David Reif, *Leksikon ratnih zločina: Ono što bi javnost trebala da zna* (trans. by Nevena Novović & Milutin Marjanov, orig. *Crimes of War. What the Public Should Know* (1999)). Beograd: Samizdat B92, pp. 123–126.

Curtois, Stéphane. 2007. Črna knjiga komunizma: več kot 90 milijonov mrtvih. In: Bernard Nežmah, *Zrcala komunizma: intervjuji 1994–2005*, Ljubljana: Modrijan, pp. 134–137.

Čepič, Zdenko, Borak, Neven & Fischer, Jasna. 2005. *Slovenska novejša zgodovina. Od programa Zedinjene Slovenije do mednarodnega priznanja Republike Slovenije. 1848–1992* (*Slovenian recent history*), Vol. 2, Ljubljana: Mladinska knjiga.

Dežman, Jože. 2008. Tranzicijska pravičnost (Transitional justice). In: J. Dežman (ed.), *Poročilo Komisije Republike Slovenije za reševanje vprašanj prikritih grobišč 2005–2008 (Report of the Commission of the Republic of Slovenia for solving the questions regarding the concealed mass graves 2005–2008)*, Ljubljana: Družina, pp. 266–269.

Dolinar, France M. 1998. Katoliška cerkev v Sloveniji po drugi svetovni vojni (The Catholic church in Slovenia after the Second World War). In: D. Jančar (ed.), *Temna stran meseca: kratka zgodovina totalitarizma v Sloveniji 1945–1990* (*The dark side of the Moon: a short history of totalitarianism in Slovenia 1945–1990*), Ljubljana: Nova revija, pp. 222–233.

Dreyfus, H. L. 2004. Heidegger's Ontology of Art. In Dreyfus, H. L. & Wrathall, M. A. (eds.), *A Companion to Heidegger*. Oxford UK & Cambridge USA: Blackwell, pp. 407–419.

Dubajić, Simo Š. 2006. *Život, greh i kajanje: ispovedna autobiografska hronika. Knj. 1, Od Kistanja do Kočevskog Roga*. Novi Beograd: Vesti; Bad Vilbel: Nidda Verlag.

Dunning, Stephen N. 1985. Kierkegaard's Systematic Analysis of Anxiety. In Perkins (ed.), pp. 7–33.

Eiletz, Silvin. 2008. *Titova skrivnostna leta v Moskvi: 1935–1940* (*Tito's mysterious years in Moscow: 1935–1940*), Celovec & Ljubljana & Dunaj: Celovška Mohorjeva.

Ferenc, Mitja. 2012. Independent Slovenia and concealed mass graves. In: J. Juhant & B. Žalec (eds.) *Reconciliation: The Way of Healing and Growth*, Berlin: LIT Verlag, pp. 233–240.

Flangan, Kieran & Jupp, P. C. (eds.) 2001. *Virtue Ethics and Sociology: Issues of Modernity and Religion*, Basingstoke & New York: Palgrave Macmillan.

Fraser, Nancy. 2003. *Redistribution or Recognition? A Political-Philosophical Exchange – with A. Honneth*. London: Verso.

Freud, Sigmund. 2013. *Moses and Monotheism* (trans. Katherine Jones). Edition Kindle.

Fukuyama, Francis. 1995. *Trust: The Social Virtues and the Creation of Prosperity*, New York: Free Press.

Gabriel, Merigala. 2011. The Concept of Love in Kierkegaard and Gandhi, in Andrew J. Burgess (ed.), *Kierkegaard: East and West, Acta Kierkegaardiana,* Vol. 5, Toronto, Ontario: Kierkegaard Circle, Trinity College, University of Toronto, pp. 89–99.

Galston, William. 1991. *Liberal purposes: goods, virtues, and diversity in the liberal state*, Cambridge: Cambridge University Press.

Galston, William. 2002. *Liberal Pluralism: The Implications of Value Pluralism for Political Theory and Practice*. Cambridge: Cambridge University Press.

Gandhi, Mohandas K. 1987. *Autobiography: The Story of My Experiments with Truth* (trans. Mahadev Desai). Harmondsworth, Middlesex: Penguin Books.

Govier, Trudy. 1997. *Social Trust and Human Communities*. Montreal: McGill Queens University Press.

Granda, Stane. 2008. *Slovenija: Pogled na njeno zgodovino* (*Slovenia: A view on its history*), Ljubljana: Urad vlade za komuniciranje.

Griesser-Pečar, Tamara. 1998. Procesi proti duhovnikom in redovništvu po maju 1945 (Processes against clerics, monks and nuns after the May 1945), In: D. Jančar (ed.), *Temna stran meseca: kratka zgodovina totalitarizma v Sloveniji 1945–1990* (*The dark side of the Moon: a short history of totalitarianism in Slovenia 1945–1990*), Ljubljana: Nova revija, pp. 113–125.

Halik, Tomas. 2009. *Patience with God: The Story of Zacchaeus Continuing in Us*. New York: Doubleday.

Hall, Ronald L. 1985. Language and Freedom: Kierkegaard's Analysis of the Demonic in *The Concept of Anxiety*. In Perkins (ed.), pp. 153–166.

Hardin, Russell. 1992. The Street-Level Epistemology. *Analyse & Kritik*, 14, 2, 1992, pp. 152–176.

Hardin, Russell. 2002. *Trust and Trustworthiness*. New York: Russell Sage Foundation.

Harff, Barbara. 2003. No Lessons Learned from the Holocaust? Assesing Risks of Genocide and Political Mass Murder since 1995. In: *American Political Science Review*, February, 97: 1, pp. 57–73.

Hartmann, Richard. 2008. Chances and Limits of Dialogue in a Globalized World. In: J. Juhant & B. Žalec (eds), *Surviving Globalization: The Uneasy Gift of Interdependence,* Münster: LIT Verlag, pp. 95–106.

Haugeland, John. 1995. Dasein's Disclosedness. In Dreyfus, H. L. & Harisson, H. (eds.), *Heidegger: A Critical Reader*. Oxford UK & Cambridge USA: Blackwell, pp. 27–44.

Havel, Václav. 1985. The power of powerless. In: John Keane (ed.), *The Power of Powerless: Citizens Against the State in Central-Eastern Europe*. New York: M. E. Sharpe, pp. 23–96.

Heidenrich, John G. 2001. *How to Prevent Genocide: A Guide for Policymakers, Scholars, and the Concerned Citizen*. Westport, Connecticut in London: Praeger.

Herbert, David. 2001. Virtue Ethics, Justice and Religion in Multicultural Societies. In Flanagan, K. and Jupp, P. C. (eds.), *Virtue Ethics and Sociology: Issues of Modernity and Religion,* pp. 51–67.

Hollennbach, David S. J. 2003. *The Common Good and Christian Ethics*. Cambridge (UK): Cambridge University Press.

Hribar, Tine. 1987. Kierkegaardovski suspenz. In: Sören A. Kierkegaard, *Ponovitev*; *Filozofske drobtinice ali Drobec filozofije* (trans. Franc Burgar), Ljubljana: Slovenska matica, pp. 233–272.

Hribar, Tine. 2004. *Euroslovenstvo* (*Euroslovenianism*), Ljubljana: SM.

Igličar, Albin. 2011. Sociološko-pravni vidiki Slovenije kot pravne in demokratične države (Sociological and legal aspects of Slovenia as a democratic state governed by the rule of law). *Dignitas*, 13, 51–52, pp. 58–76.

Inkret, Andrej. 2011. *In stoletje bo zardelo*. Ljubljana: Modrijan.

Irigaray, Luce. 2004. *Key Writings*. London & New York: Continuum.

Jančar, Drago. 1998a. Temna stran meseca (The dark side of the Moon). In: D. Jančar (ed.), *Temna stran meseca: kratka zgodovina totalitarizma v Sloveniji 1945–1990* (*The dark side of the Moon: a short history of totalitarianism in Slovenia 1945–1990*), Ljubljana: Nova revija.

Jančar, Drago. 1998b. Čemu ta knjiga, čemu razstava (Why this book, why this exhibition). In: D. Jančar (ed.), *Temna stran meseca: kratka zgodovina totalitarizma v Sloveniji 1945–1990* (*The dark side of the Moon: a short history of totalitarianism in Slovenia 1945–1990*), Ljubljana: Nova revija, pp. 383–386.

Jones, Adam. 2011 [2006]. *Genocide: A Comprehensive Introduction*. London & New York: Routledge.

Juhant, Janez. 2002. Globalisation and Anthropology. In: *Anthropological Notebooks*, Vol. VIII, No. 1, pp. 41–51.

Juhant, Janez. 2008. *Im Feuer der europäischen Ideenzüge: Slowenien*, Wien & Zürich & Berlin & Münster: LIT Verlag.

Juhant, Janez. 2010. *Idejni spopad II: katoličani in revolucija (The clash of ideas II: Catholics and Revolution)*. Ljubljana: Teološka fakulteta.

Kierkegaard, Søren. 1962. *The Point of View for My Work as an Author* (trans. Walter Lowrie). New York: Harper and Row.

Kierkegaard, Søren. 1980. *The Concept of Anxiety* (trans. Reidar Thomte). Princeton: Princeton University Press.

Kierkegaard, Søren. 1985. *The Sickness Unto Death* (trans. Howard W. Hong and Edna H. Hong). Princeton: Princeton University Press.

Kierkegaard, Søren. 2012. *The Soul of Kierkegaard: Selections from His Journals*. Edited and introduction by Alexander Dru. Edition Kindle.

Killingsworth, Matt. *Civil Society in Communist Eastern Europe: Opposition and Dissent in Totalitarian Regimes*. Colchester: ECPR Press 2012.

Kleyman, Mark. 2012. Urban development, grassroots authoritarianism and the problem of reconciliation in post-Soviet Russia. In Juhant, J. and Žalec, B. (eds.), *Reconciliation: The Way of Healing and Growth*. Berlin: Lit, pp. 241–248.

Kogovšek Šalomon, Neža. 2012. *Izbris in (ne)ustavna demokracija* (Erasure and (non)constitutional democracy). Ljubljana: GV Založba.

Kossoff, Philip. 1983. *Valiant Heart: A Biography of Heinrich Heine*. London: Cornwall Books.

Küng, Hans. 1991. *Projekt Weltethos*. München: Piper.

Kuper, Leo. 1981. *Genocide: Its Political Use in Twentieth Century*. Harmondsworth: Penguin.

Kymlicka, Will. 1995. *Multicultural Citizenship: A Liberal Theory of Minority Rights*. Oxford: Clarendon Press.

Kymlicka, Will. 2000 [2002]. *Contemporary Political Philosophy: An Introduction*. Oxford: Oxford University Press.

Lemkin, Raphael. 1944. *Axis Rule in Occupied Europe: Laws of Occupation, Analysis of Government, Proposals for Redress*. Washington DC: Carnegie Endowment for International Peace, Division of International Law.

Leenaars, A. A. 2005. Trauma and Suicide among Aboriginal People: Stories from the Arctic and Australia (with Particular Reference to the Situation in Lithuania). In: D. Gailienė (ed.), *The Psychology of Extreme Traumatization: The Aftermath of Political Repression*, Vilnius: Akreta.

Levi, Primo. 2003. *Potopljeni in rešeni* (trans. by Irena Prosenc Šegula, orig. *I sommersi e i salvati*). Ljubljana: Studia humanitatis.

Levy, J. T. 2000. *The Multiculturalism of Fear*. New York: Oxford University Press.

Lewis, J. D. & Weigert, Andrew. 1985. Trust as a social reality. *Social Forces*, 63, 4, pp. 967–985.

Lorey, David E. & Beezley, William H. 2002. Introduction. In: David E. Lorey & William H. Beezley, *Genocide, Collective Violence and Popular Memory: The Politics of Remembrance in the Twentieth Century*. Wilmington, Delaware: SR Books, pp. xi–xxxiii.

Luckmann, Thomas. 1990. Social Communication, Dialogue and Conversation. In: I. Markova and K. Foppa (eds.), *The Dynamics of Dialogue*, New York: Harvester Wheatsheaf, pp. 45–61.

Luhmann, Niklas. 1979. *Trust and Power*. New York: Wiley

Luthar, Breda & Luthar, Oto. 2003. Monopolization of memory: the politics and textuality of war memorials in Slovenia after 1991. *European Perspectives*, Vol. 5, No. 18.

Măcelaru, Marcel. 2012. Babel from Text to Symbol: Possibilities of Reconciliation in the Hebrew Bible. In Juhant, J. and Žalec, B. (eds.), *Reconciliation: The Way of Healing and Growth*. Berlin: Lit, pp. 51–58.

MacIntyre, Alasdair. 1999. *Dependent Rational Animals: Why Human Beings Need the Virtues*. Chicago: Open Court.

MacIntyre, Alasdair. 2006. Toleration and the goods of conflict. In MacIntyre, A., *Ethics and Politics: Selected Essays, Volume 2*. Cambridge: Cambridge University Press, pp. 205–223.

MacIntyre, Alasdair. 2000. *After Virtue: A Study in Moral Theory*. London: Duckworth.

Maier, Hans (ed.) 2004. *Totalitarianism and political religions. Vol. 1, Concepts for the comparison of dictatorship* (trans. by Jodi Bruhn). London, New York: Routledge.

Mann, Michael. 2005. *The Dark Side of Democracy: Explaining Ethnic Cleansing*. Cambridge: Cambridge University Press.

Margalit, Avishai. 2009. *On Compromise and Rotten Compromises*. Princeton, N.J.: Princeton University Press.

Martinjak, Ana. 2010. Teorija Hannah Arendt o totalitarizmu (Hannah Arendt's theory of totalitarianism). In: *Anthropos*, Year 42, No. 3–4, pp. 271–294.

McLeod, Carolyn. 2011. Trust. In: *Stanford Encyclopedia of Philosophy*, accessible at http://plato.stanford.edu/entries/trust/ (June 15th, 2011).

Michéa, Jean-Claude. 2009. *The Realm of Lesser Evil*. Malden: Polity Press.

Mieth, Dietmar. 2008. The Role and Backgrounds of Religious Ethical, Legal and Social Issues in the Progress of Science. In Juhant, J. & Žalec, B. (eds.), *Surviving Globalization: The Uneasy Gift of Interdependence*, Münster: Lit, pp. 149–161.

Neumann, Franz. 1964. Notes on the Theory of Dictatorship. In: Franz Neumann, *The Democratic and the Authoritarian State: Essays in Political and Legal Theory*. Edited and with a Preface by Herbert Marcuse. London: The Free Press of Glencoe, pp. 233–256.

Nickel, James W. 2001. Moral Dimensions of Four Ways of Getting Rid of Groups. In: Jokić, A. (ed.). *War Crimes and Collective Wrongdoing: A Reader*. Malden, MA: Blackwell, pp. 163–175.

Nozick, Robert. 1974. *Anarchy, State and Utopia*. Oxford: Oxford University Press, pp. 25–73.

Pahor, Boris in Rebula, Alojz. 1975. *Edvard Kocbek – pričevalec našega časa*. Trst: Zaliv.

Patterson, Orlando. 1982. *Slavery and Social Death: A Comparative Study*. Cambridge, MA: Harvard University Press.

Perkins, Robert L. (ed.) 1985. *International Kierkegaard Commentary: The Concept of Anxiety*. Macon, Georgia: Mercer University Press.

Pirjevec, Jože. 1995. *Jugoslavija: Nastanek, razvoj ter razpad Karadjordjevićeve in Titove Jugoslavije* (*Yugoslavia: the rise, development and downfall of Karadjordjevic's and Tito's Yugoslavia*). Koper: Lipa.

Pope John Paul II. 2005. *Memory & Identity: Personal Reflections*. London: Weidenfeld & Nicolson.

Pučnik, Jože. 1998. Množični povojni poboji (Mass killings after the war). In: D. Jančar (ed.), *Temna stran meseca: kratka zgodovina totalitarizma v Sloveniji 1945–1990* (*The dark side of the moon: a short history of totalitarianism in Slovenia 1945–1990*), Ljubljana: Nova revija.

Putnam R. D. (together with R. Leonardi & R. Nanetti) 1993. *Making Democracy Work: Civic Traditions in Modern Italy*. Princeton: Princeton University Press.

Putnam, Hilary. 2008. *Capabilities and Two Ethical Theories*. In *Journal of Human Development*, Vol. 9, No. 3, pp. 377–388.

Rae, Murray. 2010. *Kierkegaard and Theology*. London in New York: T&T Clark International.

Rawls, John. 1993. *Political Liberalism*. New York: Columbia University Press.

Repar, Primož. 1998. Tesnoba eksistence in eksistencialna komunikacija. In S. Kierkegaard, *Pojem tesnobe: preprosto psihološko nazorno razmišljanje v smeri dogmatičnega problema izvirnega greha* (trans. Primož Repar). Ljubljana: Slovenska matica, pp. 223–290.

Rothstein, Bo. 2000. Trust, Social Dilemmas and Collective Memories. *Journal of Theoretical Politics*, 12, 4, pp. 477–501,

Sartre, Jean-Paul. 1976. *Critique of Dialectical Reason I: Theory of Practical Ensembles* (trans. by Alan Sheridan-Smith). London: NLB.

Schlesinger Jr., Arthur. 1998. *The Disunity of America: Reflections on a Multicultural Society*, rev. edn. New York: W. W. Norton.

Schmemann, Serge. 2003. Terorizam protiv civila (Terrorism against civilians). In: Roy Guttman & David Reif, *Leksikon ratnih zločina: Ono što bi javnost trebala da zna* (trans. by N. Novović & M. Marjanov, orig. *Crimes of War. What the Public Should Know* (1999)). Beograd: Samizdat B92, pp. 478–479.

Schwab, Philipp. 2012. *Der Rückstoß der Methode: Kierkegaard und die indirekte Mitteilung*. Berlin/Boston: Walter de Gruyter.

Sen, Amartya. 1999. Democracy as Universal Value. *Journal of Democracy*, 10, 3, pp. 3–17.

Sen, Amartya. 2007. *Identity and Violence: The Illusion of Destiny*. New York & London: W. W. Norton & Company.

Siedentop, Larry. 2000 [2001]. *Democracy in Europe*, London: Allen Lane.

Simoniti, Vasko. 1998. Permanentna revolucija, totalitarizem, strah (Permanent revolution, totalitarianism, fear). In: D. Jančar (ed.), *Temna stran meseca: kratka zgodovina totalitarizma v Sloveniji 1945–1990* (*The dark side of the Moon: a short history of totalitarianism in Slovenia 1945–1990*), Ljubljana: Nova revija, pp. 39–52.

Slootweg, Timo J. M. 2009. Love and Violence: Dialectical Reflection on the Phenomenology of Crusade. In: Bart C. Labuschagne & Reinhard W. Sonnenschmidt (ed.), *Religion, Politics and Law: Philosophical Reflections on the Sources of Normative Society*, Leiden, Boston: Brill, pp. 223–256.

Solomon, Robert C. & Flores, Fernando. 2003. *Building Trust: In Business, Politics, Relationships, and Life*. Oxford: Oxford University Press.

St. Augustine. *S. Aurelii Augustini opera omnia: patrologiae latinae elenchus*. Available at: http://www.augustinus.it/latino/ (July 24th, 2011).

Strahovnik, Vojko. 2011. Identity, Character and Ethics. In: *Synthesis Philosophica*, 51, Vol. 26, Fasc. 1, pp. 67–77.

Sunderland, Margot. 2006. *The Science of Parenting*, London: DK Adult.

Šturm, Lovro. 1998. O kratenju človekovih pravic in temeljnih svoboščin v obdobju 1945–1998 (Violation of human rights and basic liberties in Slovenia from 1945 to 1990). In: D. Jančar (ed.), *Temna stran meseca: kratka zgodovina totalitarizma v Sloveniji 1945–1990* (*The dark side of the Moon: a short history of totalitarianism in Slovenia 1945–1990*), Ljubljana: Nova revija, pp. 65–112.

Taylor, Charles. 1994. The Politics of Recognition. In Gutmann, A. (ed.), *Multiculturalism: Examining the Politics of Recognition*. Princeton, New Jersey: Princeton University Press.

Todorov, Tzvetan. 2012. *Totalitarna izkušnja (Totalitarian experience)* (trans. Veronika Simoniti). Maribor: Hiša knjig, Založba KMŠ.

Toš, Niko et al. 1990. SJM90/2 – Stališča Slovencev o ustavi (Standpoints of Slovenians about the constitution). Ljubljana: SJM. Accessible at:http://www.cjm.si/sites/cjm.si/files/File/e-dokumenti/SJM_vrednote_v_prehodu_2.pdf (January 2nd, 2012).

Trigg, Roger. 2007. *Religion in Public Life: Must Faith Be Privatized?* Oxford: Oxford University Press.

Udayakumar, S. P. 1995. The Futures of the Poor. *Futures*, 27, 3, pp. 339–351.

Uslaner, Eric. 2008. Trust as a Moral Value. In: D. Castiglione & J. W. van Deth & G. Wolleb (eds.), *The Handbook of Social Capital*, Oxford: Oxford University Press, pp. 101–121.

Voegelin, Eric. 1987. *The New Science of Politics: An Introduction*. Chicago & London: The University of Chicago Press.

Volf, Miroslav. 2011. "Honor everyone!": Christian faith and the culture of universal respect. In Volf, M., Constantineanu, C., Măcelaru, M. and K. Šimič (eds.), *First the Kingdom of God: A* Festschrift *in Honor of Prof. Dr. Peter Kuzmič*. Osijek: Evanđeoski teološki fakultet, pp. 3–32.

Walzer, Michael. 1990. The Communitarian Critique of Liberalism. *Political Theory* 18, 1, pp. 6–23.

Walzer, Michael. 1997. *On Toleration*. New Haven and London: Yale University Press.

Walzer, Michael. 2004. *Politics and Passion: Toward a More Egalitarian Liberalism*. New Haven and London: Yale University Press.

Weiler, J. H. H. 2003. *Un' Europa Cristiana*. Milano: Biblioteca Universale Rizzoli.

Yankelovich, Daniel. 2001. *The Magic of Dialogue: Transforming Conflict into Cooperation*, New York: Touchstone.

Young, Iris Marion. 1990. *Justice and the Politics of Difference*. Princeton, NJ: Princeton University Press.

Young, Iris Marion. 1997. *Intersecting Voices: Dilemmas of Gender, Political Philosophy, and Policy*. Princeton, NJ: Princeton University Press.

Žalec, Bojan. 2007. Civic virtue and modern pluralistic liberal democracy. In Hünermann, P., Juhant, J., Žalec, B. (eds.), *Dialogue and Virtue: Ways to Overcome Clashes of Our Civilizations*, Münster: Lit, pp. 47–56.

Žalec, Bojan. 2008. Possibilities of a universalistic ethics: the capabilities approach. In Juhant, J., Žalec, B. (eds.). *Surviving Globalization: The Uneasy Gift of Interdependence*. Berlin: Lit, pp. 33–58.

Žalec, Bojan. 2011a. Personalism, truth and human rights. In: Janez Juhant and Bojan Žalec (eds.), *Humanity after Selfish Prometheus: Chances of Dialogue and Ethics in a Technicized World*. Münster: Lit, pp. 29–41.

Žalec, Bojan. 2011b. On not knowing who we are: the ethical importance of transcendent anthropology. In: *Synthesis Philosophica*, 51, vol. 26, fasc. 1, pp. 105–115.

Žalec, Bojan. 2011c. Dejavniki genocida, njegovo preprečevanje in etika soočenja z njim (Factors of genocide, its preventing and ethics of facing it). In: Jože Dežman (ed.), *Resnica in sočutje: prispevki k črni knjigi titoizma. Poročilo 3: poročilo Komisije Vlade RS za reševanje vprašanj prikritih grobišč 2009–2011* (Truth and compassion: contributions to the black book of Titoism). Ljubljana: Družina, pp. 299–314.

Žalec, Bojan. 2011d. Nezaupanje kot ključni dejavnik slabega delovanja skupnosti, organizacij in družbe (Mistrust as the key factor of malfunction of community, organizations and society). *Dignitas*, 13, 51–52, pp. 351–373.

Žižek, Slavoj. 2005. Against Human Rights. *New Left Review* 34 (July–August), pp. 115–131.

Resources

Žalec, Bojan. 2012. The case of Slovenia from the point of view of the theory of citizenship. *Archiwum historii filozofii i myśli społecznej = Archive of the history of philosophy and social thought*. Vol. 57, pp. 129–149.

Žalec, Bojan. 2012b Multiculturalism, liberalism and Christianity: some elucidations (concerning Europe). In: Podunavac, Milan (ed.), *Challenges of multiculturalism* Beograd: Heinrich Böll Foundation, pp. 141–160.

Žalec, Bojan. 2013. Genocide as social death: A comparative conceptual analysis. *Anthropological Notebooks*, 19 (2), pp. 57–74.

Žalec, Bojan. 2014. Nazism and Stalinism in the light of Kierkegaard's thought. *Filozofia*, 69, 5, pp. 443–450.

ABSTRACT

This book is a philosophical book. It consists of four main essays. It deals with rather delicate subjects like genocide, totalitarianism and multiculturalism. The author considers these topics at several levels. The first essay is in a sense the most central. It brings a detailed analysis of the concept of genocide as social death. A debt to Claudia Card is evident. The second brings the reflection in the light of Kierkegaardian concepts of anxiety and stadia of existence by means of which he reflects on Nazism and Stalinism. A debt to work of Charles K. Bellinger in this endeavour is obvious. The third essay deals at length with different concept(ion)s of multiculturalism. The author points to the unacceptable consequences of the implementation of multiculturalism understood as axiological levelling of all cultures. Strong influence of ideas of Larry Siedentop in this paper can't be denied. The most concrete essay in the book is the last one where the author applies the concepts of the theory of citizenship to enlighten the Slovene story. This essay brings also concrete data about rather bloody recent history of Slovenia which is however not very well known outside this country. The main methodological principle of the author is that the job of a philosopher – and philosophical creativity – consists in either introducing new concepts, without which our thinking is inferior, or in their illuminative application. The view which the author named solidary personalism represents the background of all thinking in this book and the basic ethical measure. Christian faith and (intellectual) tradition, works of Kierkegaard, Franz Brentano, Emmanuel Mounier, Hannah Arendt, but also of Nikolay Berdiaev, Martin Buber, France Veber, Milan Komar, Eric Voegelin, Alasdair MacIntyre, Charles Taylor, Martha Nussbaum, Luce Irigaray, Martin Heidegger, Hubert Dreyfus, Emmanuel Lévinas, Zygmunt Bauman, Will Kymlicka, Wittgenstein and some parts of analytical tradition are among its main origins, examples and inspirations.

ABOUT THE AUTHOR

Bojan Žalec, PhD is an Associate Professor of Philosophy, a Senior Research Fellow and the Head of the Institute of Philosophy and Social Ethics at the Faculty of Theology, University of Ljubljana. He studied philosophy, sociology, mathematics and theology. As a postgraduate student he spent one year in Würzburg, Germany (Franz Brentano Institute). He was visiting Professor at the Faculty of Theology of University of Zagreb, and a visiting researcher at the Polish Academy of Science in Warsaw. He is the author of many books and articles published in several languages. In his work he combines the classical and Christian philosophical tradition with phenomenology, findings of analytical philosophy and its forerunners (especially Wittgenstein, Davidson, externalism (Putnam) and critique of classical foundationalism (Plantinga) should be mentioned). In the areas of ethics and political philosophy he stresses the importance of recognition of transcendence (of human person), virtues, dialogue and solidarity. The works of thinkers like Hannah Arendt, Eric Voegelin, Alasdair MacIntyre, Charles Taylor, Martha Nussbaum and also Zygmunt Bauman represent the main origin and frame of reference of his research in those regions. He introduced the term *solidary personalism* (as opposed to nihilism and instrumentalism) to denote the principal background of his thought. As a coeditor and as a coauthor he has published eight books in English – all by Lit Verlag – which deal with faith and science, dialogue, globalization, chances of ethics and humanity in a technicized world, reconciliation, culture of fear, and related topics. In preparation is a book on suicide and genocide.

Address:
Faculty of Theology
Poljanska c. 4
SI–1000 Ljubljana
SLOVENIA
E-mail: bojan.zalec@guest.arnes.si